# End
# Silenced
# Abuse
## Tell Somebody

## ALEESHA BARLOW
### WITH SHALONDA SJ JOHNSON

THE TMG FIRM

*New York*

The TMG Firm, LLC
112 W. 34th Street
17th and 18th Floors
New York, NY 10120
www.thetmgfirm.com

Published by The TMG Firm, LLC

For more information about special discounts for bulk purchase, please
contact The TMG Firm at 1-888-984-3864 ext 12 or
publishing@thetmgfirm.com

ISBN: 978-0-99879-933-9
Library of Congress Control Number: 2017954838
All rights reserved

First The TMG Firm Trade Paperback Edition October 2017
Printed in the United States of America

This is a work of creative nonfiction. The events are portrayed to the best of
Aleesha Barlow's memory. The conversations in this book all come from the
author's recollections, though they are not written to represent word-for-
word transcripts. Rather, the author has retold them in a way that evokes the
feeling and meaning what was said and in all instances, the essence of the
dialogue is accurate. While all the stories in this book are true, some names
and identifying details have been changed to protect the privacy of the
people involved.

Cover created and designed by Brittani Williams for
TSPub Creative, LLC.

I dedicate this book to my dad. You helped me start my *Tell Somebody* movement, and I love you so much for that. Before you passed away, you told me that you were proud of me for advocating against sexual abuse because somebody had to do it. You were right and that somebody is me. That's why I do it every day! As you look down on me from heaven, I hope I continue to make you proud every step of the way.

The second person I dedicate this book to is my daughter Kalani. You were only five-years-old when we started this journey, and I appreciate your dedication. You've been right by my side at speaking engagements, wearing the *Tell Somebody* clothes to school, educating your friends and helping me save lives. I know when you're older you're going to do even more wonderful things with this movement. And I'm going to be there with you helping you along the way.

I also dedicate this book to all survivors of sexual abuse. It's time to tell somebody so you can heal. It's time to use your story to help others. I'm a living example that it can be done, you're strong, you can do it...I believe in you.

To Ms. Oprah Winfrey, thank you for the kind words and acknowledging my strength to triumph through. Because of you, I will continue to support others who have faced what I have. Thank you, Leah Rex and The TMG Firm family for believing in my story. I firmly believe this will empower and touch the lives of many others.

Last but not least, I dedicate this to all of the children who are going through any type of abuse at this very moment. I know you need a voice, and I'm here to be that for you. I pray every night that you build enough strength to tell somebody. I pray that God gives you the strength, courage, and wisdom to tell somebody. And when you do, I pray they act immediately.

# PREFACE

*Child sexual abuse is a form of abuse in which an adult or older adolescent uses a child for sexual stimulation.*

If I were told at the age of six that by the time I was thirty-one, I would be the CEO of an organization called Tell Somebody and an advocate against sexual abuse; I would have never believed it. Yet, I am that person. To this day I am still in recovery and on the road to healing; fighting to get back my strength by helping one person at a time. Child abuse is often hard to detect because victims rarely speak up. And when they do, the incident is often downplayed. I was that person, that little girl who didn't say anything and when I did, I was silenced. I never could have imagined that someone that loved me so much could extend a great deal of pain at the same time.

I'm here to give voice to the secrets of my grandfather's pedophilic ways and heal the pain dealt by someone so dear to me. It's my duty to take the blaming finger that I once pointed at myself and direct it toward the rightful owner. That person is none other than my grandfather, Theodorus Bernardus Dejong. He emotionally and physically molested me from the age of six to fourteen-years-old. His curiosity and fascination with my six-year-old body grew increasingly disturbing. Though I will never understand his reasoning, he derived pleasure from keeping his hands in my underwear. He stole my innocence, a part of me that I will never get back. He left me with a childhood that's worth forgetting, yet I can't. I will never be able to escape the memories of forced sexual abuse at the hands of a man I once admired. Regardless of how hard I try to forget, that experience will be with me forever. But even though I will live with what he did to me, I have vowed to free myself from the pain and embarrassment that his heinous acts left behind. I'm no longer giving him power over my life. I am breaking the so-called special bond he said we shared and giving myself a brand new outlook on life. I hope the details of my abuse will inspire someone to find the strength and voice needed to end silenced abuse.

# CHAPTER ONE

Born on June 13, 1986, to parents of Dutch and African-American descent, I always considered myself a typical 'California' girl having grown up just forty minutes outside of San Francisco in Foster City. My parents' differing cultures clashed at times, but love always outweighed any difference in opinion. For example, my parents had varied approaches to discipline. Timeout is the most fitting label for my mother's go-to disciplinary action. On those occasions when I got into mischief or rebelled, I earned thirty to forty-five minutes of alone time with my confidant, the corner. It gave just enough time to gripe about everything that pissed me off from having been scolded and my mother's audacity to put me in time out.

Being disciplined by my father...let's just say it was a bit different. He was very stern and stood firm on how he felt his children should behave. He did not consider timeouts to be the most effective form of discipline. Just hearing his strong masculine baritone voice straightened me out in seconds. He spoke with conviction and expected respectful, well-behaved children. Although my parents were different ethnicities, life growing up never seemed black or white to me; I guess you can say I saw things in gray. People were just people, and before the traumatic sexual abuse happened, I was just a little girl full of life searching and hoping to find nothing but happiness.

I'm the second oldest of five. I have an older brother named Charles, from my father's previous marriage, a younger brother named Jayson, who shares the same mother and father as I, and two younger brothers from my father whom I met when I was fourteen. Before Jayson was born, I sometimes felt like I was an only child. Charles was much older and wasn't at home regularly, so it was often just my mother, father, and I.

My family spoiled me to no end, and there was nothing that I asked for that I did not receive. Going to the toy store was like a religious ritual for me. Before setting one foot into the store, I sent silent prayers up to God asking that the latest Baby Alive and Barbie dolls were in stock, on the shelves and ready for purchase. It wasn't before long that my mother naturally incorporated stopping for toys into her routine. I would walk up and down the aisles, admiring every single toy. I took the time to inspect every one of them to determine if they were worthy of joining the other toys that invaded majority of the space in my room. There was no discrimination based on gender, just because a toy was advertised for boys didn't mean that I couldn't find a purpose for it once I got home. I would grab as much as my short, chubby arms could carry and met my mother at the front of the store to fill her cart with what would soon be my prized possessions.

Being in the toy store felt like I was in my own world; one filled with Barbies and Cabbage Patch Kids. I was in a bubble full of fantasy that would soon burst, and force me into the harsh reality of sexual abuse.

My mother and father weren't the only family members who spoiled me with gifts; my maternal grandfather also played a significant role. Even though my mother occasionally worked alongside my grandfather at his insurance agency and my father was a retired Air Force veteran with a job at the post office, they would every so often fall on hard times. My grandfather, being well-off, was always there to contribute financially or in whatever other way was needed to keep my parents afloat and provide me with a life of rewards.

I now know all of the presents and perks came with a price. My grandfather paid special attention to me and gave me whatever I wanted. Christmas was my favorite time of the year, and it never ceased to amaze me how he managed to pack hundreds of gifts under our Christmas tree. Each year, there were so many gifts crowded across the living room floor that we barely had anywhere to sit. Filled with excitement, I would open one gift while eyeing the next gift. It was common for me to receive two hundred fifty dollar game systems with multiple fifty dollar games, dolls, doll houses, and whatever else I desired. My grandfather made me happy; he was my idol and besides my father, was my hero. He and I were inseparable, and I would follow him wherever he went. In return he made me feel like the most special girl in the world. There are many pictures of us smiling, as he hugged or held me. My love for him was unmatched. He reciprocated the love I expressed for him by making sure to put a smile on my face and teaching me new things. One thing, in particular, he liked to teach me was how to play the piano, which was my favorite pastime. As we played, he gave me a look of admiration as he complimented my perfectly elongated fingers. He always said they were perfect for being a pianist. To the naked eye, it just looked like admiration from a grandfather to a granddaughter and nothing more.

Hearing the loud bang or ding sound, depending on what key I stroked, gave me a sense of excitement even if the noise didn't develop into beautiful music. Not knowing his true intentions, I enjoyed the love and affection I received from him. But as I think back his admiring, luring stares said it all and set the stage for what was soon to come.

My grandfather was everything to me, and I loved visiting my grandparents. They were upper class and had a few homes, three that I specifically remember. Their first home was about five minutes away from us in Foster City. After which they moved to a new home in Roseville, about two and a half hours away. My grandparents even had a vacation home in Lake Almanor, which is in the northeastern part of California, approximately four hours from Foster City.

When they lived in Foster City, my grandparents stayed close enough to us that they were the perfect babysitters, so I spent a lot of time there. In the beginning, it never bothered me to go to their house. Whenever I was told of my visits, I became excited and overjoyed just thinking of all of the fun things my grandfather and I were going to do. The best part of it all was that my grandfather always allowed me to choose the activities. I would be quite indecisive, to say the least, because I wanted to do everything. One visit in the Spring of 1992 was different; it wasn't like all the others. This visit set the stage for all of my future visits.

When we pulled up to my grandparents' house, I had a burst of energy. I eagerly exited my mom's red Ford Thunderbird in record speed, so I could repeatedly ring their doorbell until one of them answered. With my feet firmly on the light brown welcome mat, I waited to be greeted. Just like any other six-year-old, I couldn't keep still, so I used the opportunity to attempt to catch one of the many colorful butterflies that flew around my grandmother's perfectly potted plants. My grandmother, Connie Dejong, had what people called a green thumb. She took pride in knowing that she could make any plant grow and any flower bloom to perfection with just the right care and attention.

Once the door swung open, I was met, much like I typically was, with hugs and kisses. My small stature gave me the illusion that their house was a mansion, even though it was a modern upscale two-story duplex condominium. Inside the house was in its usual immaculate state with nothing out of place. Their house had all of the amenities, but the two flights of light brown carpeted stairs lead me to three of my favorite rooms, and one of which was my grandparent's room. The light brown bamboo furniture gave their room a calm California appeal. They had a set of tall dressers; on top of one sat a statue of Buddha. I use to be amazed while looking at it, staring at his enormous belly and the necklace he wore draped around his neck.

My grandfather's home office was another favorite. That's where I would practice my banking skills. I would prop myself up in his office chair and play bank; pretending to be a teller. I would sit up straight and type on the keyboard of his computer with a rhythmic speed and pretend to cash checks from imaginary customers, portrayed by none other than my dolls.

My bedroom was my third favorite. It was amazing and felt like home away from home. It was everything I could ask for and more. The white walls were covered with pictures of cats, which were my grandmother's favorite animal. My full-size bed with the wicker headboard was covered with every stuffed animal and doll imaginable. I use to dive into them like my bed was the ball pit at Chuck E. Cheese. Instead of brightly colored balls, I grabbed for the stuffed animals and dolls around me. Usually, I ended up holding my Cabbage Patch with the stringy brown hair. I could stay in my room for hours and practice braiding my dolls hair, primping and prepping them for an imaginary night out. I loved my room. I used to lie in bed staring at the ceiling thinking to myself that I was in heaven. Little did I know that a string of nightmarish events would eventually turn into a hell that would last for years.

On this particular visit, after I had exhausted play time in my room, my grandmother called me for dinner. Reluctantly, I made my way down the stairs to the dinner table. As he had often done, my grandfather picked me up and sat me on his lap. I thought nothing of it as his hand rested on my lap and made its way under my dress. Considering there were others around the kitchen table, it didn't raise my childlike suspicions when he propped his hand against my vagina. It was my grandfather, my

Opa, as we said in Dutch. I was simply a little girl sitting on her grandfather's lap. The placement of his hand could have been an innocent mistake. That placement of my grandfather, Theodorus Bernardus Dejong's hand was the first of many other sexual acts that would follow.

Statistics show that children are most vulnerable and easily subjected to sexual abuse between the ages of seven to thirteen-years-old. That day, when I was excited and unable to contain my happiness because of the impromptu visit to my grandparents' house, was the day I became a statistic and lost my innocence.

# CHAPTER TWO

One in three girls and one in five boys become victims of sexual abuse each year. Three out of the four children who have experienced sexual abuse know, love and trust their abuser; therefore the abuse goes unreported. It is kept between the abuser and the victim. It is often framed as a secret to be kept between the two of them; one that will bring them closer. When in reality, it is a vicious bond that the victimizer prays never is broken. As the abuser builds the victim's trust, they begin to expose them to new things with hopes that they will comply without question. This is called grooming, to be specific, child grooming. The abuser legitimizes an emotional attachment to the child or establishes an emotional connection to their family in an effort to get the child and the family to let their guards down. Over time, the abuser takes advantage of the child's newly lowered inhibitions and trust. They then use the child's trust against them to look for the perfect time when they can coerce the child into allowing or performing sexual acts.

My grandfather did just that; he was a pro at it. Little by little, he made attempts to gain my trust and test my ability to keep a secret. His grooming tactic was the infamous twenty dollar bill that he would gently and quietly hand off to me with a slight wink as he told me, "Don't tell anyone; it's our little secret." To a six-year-old child, twenty dollars might as well have been a million. I would nod my head in agreement, and skip away with thoughts of what my first purchase would be. I had no idea that he was preparing to silence me from sharing future secrets. Once he was satisfied that I could keep a secret, his confidence grew, and the sexual acts subtly progressed.

Initially, the abuse didn't seem like abuse at all. We appeared to be playing games; simple, wholesome, and harmless games. A game that my grandfather and I often played was called, "the tickle game." Every child knows what this game entails. It's simply being tickled until you fall short of breath due to uncontrollable giggling. You turn red in an instant and squirm as your body is covered in tickles. All while praying to muster enough air to beg for mercy. And in due time, your pleas are heard, and you are released from captivity.

I knew that game all too well. I was most ticklish on my feet, and my grandfather knew it. He would hold my legs down to prevent me from moving my feet as he tickled them. Through my laughter, I still felt a sense of entrapment. It was almost a feeling of overwhelming panic from being unable to move and allowing someone else to have full control over me. I couldn't stop my grandfather from tickling me, no matter how bad I wanted him to. This feeling was a precursor to how I would eventually feel being sexually abused by him. I wasn't in control, my grandfather was.

He knew exactly what he was doing, and that's why he loved the tickle game. He would start with familiar innocent areas like my underarms, neck, and feet. These were areas he would tickle when others were around to indicate that tickling was normal. That it was deemed okay and appropriate to share between an adult and a child. Eventually, he tickled me on my stomach and legs in front of family members and friends.

It wasn't until we were alone that my grandfather's tickle game became more sexual and intimate. He no longer tickled only those areas that he would around family and friends. Our alone time was crucial for him because it allowed him to get me at my most vulnerable; which was why it was perfect for him when my grandmother left the house.

My grandmother, who I sometimes referred to as Oma, which means grandmother in Dutch, had the occupation that most women dreamed of, a stay at home wife. This was possible due to the success of my grandfather's booming insurance agency. She was in charge of maintaining her 'wifely duties,' which consisted of cooking, laundry, washing dishes, and even dusting the fine China displayed in the armoire. Overall she kept the house in pristine condition. She enjoyed the luxuries of being a stay at home wife. Even though she didn't have a job, she gave herself a list of things to do throughout her day to stay busy. Throughout the day, she frequently left the house for various reasons, which would give my grandfather ample time to explore my body as he pleased.

Oma started her mornings early with a five am run around the neighborhood. Then she was off, running errands and performing the charitable contribution of feeding the neighborhood's stray cats.

It seemed as if she was gone for hours. All the while I was at her home being sexually abused by her husband. He would take me by the hand and lead me upstairs. His heart was never set on a specific room. It was as if he mentally played a quick game of eenie meenie miney mo. Once he picked the room, he would close the door behind him and made sure to lock it before we began playing the tickle game. Protected by the privacy of the closed door, his hands traveled to new areas of my body. He tickled my breast over my clothes and we would both burst into laughter. I didn't know any better. I was never taught about my body, and what parts were inappropriate to be touched, so I thought this was normal. He would take my laughter as the green light to proceed further, and he did just that. His hands explored under my petite dress and tickled my vagina over my decorative panties. My six-year-old logic insisted that this was just a new area he would use to maintain the roar of laughter much like when he tickled me elsewhere. It never tickled when his fingers danced across my panties; I only laughed because it felt funny. His hands eventually roamed and found their place under my shirt, fondling and caressing my undeveloped breast. They made their way under my panties, his fingers moving rapidly to preserve the facade that he was still tickling me. It was as if he was attempting to savor every second, every minute as his fingers touched me in a way that no child should ever be touched. My young, undeveloped body gave my grandfather a sick sexual thrill, and he couldn't resist satisfying his unnatural, immoral urges. Conversely, the direct contact of his hands on my vagina gave me an uneasy feeling. It was as if the beautiful butterflies that flew around my grandmother's garden were in my stomach. It felt wrong to me. I didn't know what to think, but the first time it happened, I hoped that it was an isolated incident of tickling gone wrong. Or maybe that it was a failed attempt to make me happy, and I prayed I didn't have to endure that again. But it did.

Each time the *game* ended, my grandfather suddenly stopped as if the thrill was no longer there or he had enough. He would get up from the bed, take me by the hand and ask me what I wanted to do next. I always said the same thing, watch cartoons and eat my favorite breakfast consisting of an over easy egg. I loved popping the yolk and watching it ooze across my plate. It made everything better. It erased what happened and once again gave my grandfather the crown for being the best Opa.

My grandmother would return from her early morning excursions without so much as a question if something were wrong. So I would sit quietly to myself, and watch my cartoon friends until the silence was broken by either one of my grandparents.

This would soon become our occasional routine. Except for the room, everything stayed the same. Each time the door closed and locked behind us, it was clear that the tickling I was about to receive wouldn't be the one that made me laugh. I didn't want to participate in my grandfather's version of fun, but I didn't want to hurt his feelings. If the new tickle game made him happy, then I would play along as if it made me happy too.

When I returned home, after spending time with my grandparents, my mother never asked many questions about my stay. There were just vague, general questions such as "Did you have fun?" I would quickly answer without giving my response much thought; I just wanted to forget the vile things that occurred during my stay.

I never told anyone our secret. Opa always told me not to tell anyone. I kept it strictly between the two of us, just like when he gave me the hushed twenty dollar bills. The longer the abuse went on, the more I questioned if what my grandfather was doing was right. So, I asked. I told somebody and opened a Pandora's Box of emotions, lies, and secrets that plagued my family for years without resolution.

# CHAPTER THREE

By the time I was seven, my family and I moved from Foster City to a house purchased for us by my grandfather. Our new home was a little over an hour away in Fairfield. The move seemed to happen suddenly after I asked about the game Opa and I played. When it came time for me to ask my question, I was almost too nervous to utter a word. I thought the secret Opa and I shared needed to be told and hoped once I found the courage to tell, my grandfather would never tickle my private areas again. I was wrong.

The day I freed myself from my silence and tried to regain my adolescence, was the day my favorite aunt came into town from Texas. In honor of her visit, the entire family decided to take a trip to my grandparents' vacation home in Lake Almanor.

It always felt like such a long journey to get there. Even though the drive was only four hours, it felt like an eternity. The winding roads that we drove were cut through mountains and set dangerously close to steep cliffs. They were so narrow, I feared if we made one wrong turn or too quick of a swivel we would tumble over their edge. I enjoyed all of the foliage, beautiful lakes and breathtaking mountain views as I thought of all the fun I would have with my grandfather. There was so much to do at the vacation home that it was always difficult to decide what I wanted to do first. Would I ask Opa to take me fishing or to play our favorite games? Maybe we could even relax on his boat and watch the waves as their loud crashing interrupted our silly conversation. The choices seemed to be endless.

I rode with my aunt, while my mother, little brother, and the rest of my extended family followed behind. I knew I could talk to my aunt about anything and in return, she would give me the best advice. I loved her so much, and I trusted her more than my own mother. I felt safe with her. Although she didn't have any children of her own, I felt as if she treated me like I was hers. I suspected what my grandfather was doing wasn't right. Our trip was my chance to follow my gut and ask the appropriate questions, so I blurted it out like word vomit, "Is it okay for people to touch your private areas?" I could see that I struck a nerve. The expression on my aunt's face told me so. She looked in the rearview mirror and calmly asked what I meant by the question.

There was no turning back, so I replied, "Well, Opa touches my private areas. He sticks his hand in my pants and under my shirt." This was my moment of truth. I had never told anyone my secret before, this was the first time. My aunt was the first person I confided in, and I was scared and nervous. I didn't know what she was going to say. She paused for a moment, turned the music down, and with the expression of disbelief plastered across her face she said, "No, that is not okay, he's not supposed to do that. I will have a talk with him and your mom when we get to the vacation home. It won't happen again."

I was so relieved that she wasn't mad; she didn't yell or scream. She was calm, which put me at ease. I felt free. At that moment I was saved. My aunt came in and rescued me. She saved the day like a modern day Wonder Woman. I took a deep breath in and exhaled all of my anxiety away. I sat back in my seat with my newly restored state of mind and plastered a Cheshire Cat smile across my face. My mind wandered back to all of the fun we were all about to have.

My aunt and I had to make a quick stop to pick up her then boyfriend from the airport so that he could join in on all the festivities planned for Lake Almanor. The stop didn't take long, and before you knew it, we were back on the road. My daydreams of fun came to a quick and abrupt halt when I overheard my aunt tell her boyfriend verbatim what I told her. His once happy demeanor and slight smile changed. It was replaced by concern and a look of disgust, then absolute silence. His expression solidified that the games my grandfather attempted to pass off as fun, were indeed wrong. I began to wonder if it was the right decision to ask my aunt about my secret. What if I was interpreting the situation wrong? Was I mistaken? Was my mind playing tricks on me? Even with all of this running through my mind, I still felt free knowing I did the right thing by telling someone. Because in my heart, I knew what Opa did to me was wrong because I felt uncomfortable every time he touched me. The cat was out of the bag, and I began playing the waiting game to see what would come from it.

I was nervous when we finally arrived at the house in Lake Almanor. I didn't know who my aunt would choose to tell first. I rushed into the house, keeping my head lowered in hopes of going unnoticed. All of my family, including my grandfather, said "Hi" almost in unison. I threw up my hand, waved quickly, and responded with a respectful reply to the cordial greeting. I then rushed up the white wooden paneled stairs. At the top was a futon that overlooked the entire downstairs. In my attempt to be as inconspicuous as possible, I curled up on the futon, tucked my legs and wrapped my arms around my entire body. I resembled a rollie pollie. And much like the insect, I rolled into a ball because I was frightened.

Occasionally I would peek over the banister to watch my family from a distance. That's when I saw my aunt walk up to my grandfather and ask to speak with him privately outside. Ever so discreetly, my mother along with my two aunts walked with my grandfather outside. They traveled downhill and walked one of the many trails of Lake Almanor. I watched them through the window. My eyes followed them until they disappeared from sight. While they were gone my grandmother was in the kitchen cooking, and my little brother was aimlessly running around the house without a care in the world. I watched and lived vicariously through him while I sat and waited. They were gone for a long time, but I stayed in place; waiting and petrified of the unknown.

"What was going to happen?" I kept asking myself. The feeling of betrayal I felt for telling on my grandfather had me on the verge of tears. I didn't want to cause trouble for him or bring problems to my family. Or worst of all split the family up. I stayed huddled in the fetal position and anxiously awaited their return. It wasn't until I heard voices that I bounced up and peeked out of the window. I saw my grandfather and his three daughters walk up the hill and eventually up the driveway. My heart began to race, if I had known what a heart attack was at that time, I would have positively believed that I was extremely close to having one. Every step they took toward the house made a thump in my chest so loud you would have thought someone was purposely pounding on my chest.

As they got closer to the door, I jumped back onto the futon burrowing my head deep into the cushion. I was nervous but, at the same time, I needed to see their facial expressions to determine who was mad. I secretly wished for telepathic powers to read each of their minds to prepare for the talk I was sure we were going to have. The doorknob turned, and they all walked in. To my surprise, when I took the chance to peek over the railing, everyone appeared as if nothing had happened. No one talked about my secret; instead, they all found different topics of conversations. I was shocked. Not one of them looked like they had just finished a very serious discussion. Still afraid to look my family in the eyes, I slowly walked down the stairs. When I gathered the strength to lift my head the first face I saw was my grandfather's. He seemed very unbothered. He wasn't mad nor did he scowl at me as I had expected he would. Rather he wore an eerily calm expression. The atmosphere of the room was happy and relaxed. There was no tension in the room whatsoever, and everyone pranced around the house like my secret was just a big misunderstanding. Later in the evening we gathered at the kitchen table and ate dinner like a big happy family.

For the rest of the vacation, which lasted about four days, things went on as if nothing happened. My secret seemed to be dismissed. Presumably, everyone believed that if no one talked about it, it would eventually fade away. My grandfather didn't touch me or expose himself to me over the course of our vacation. I thought maybe the games were ending. I was happy that it was going to stop, even if none of the adults had a conversation with me.

When we returned home from Lake Almanor, my mother pulled me into her room and told me that she heard what happened. She continued on to tell me that during their walk, her and my aunts confronted my grandfather. He admitted to them that he was indeed touching me, but it was only because my grandmother had stopped having sexual relations with him. So to fulfill his sexual needs and desires, he molested me. She told me that he followed his confession with the declaration that the devil led him to commit the heinous acts. My aunt's solution was to give him a Bible with the insistence he read it daily for guidance and strength to resist his urge to touch me. According to her, my grandfather then looked them all in their eyes and said he would never touch me again.

At the age of six, I didn't know the legal ramifications of my grandfather's actions, but his punishment seemed like a slap on the wrist. At his leisure, their father enjoyed fondling, caressing and playing with his six-year-old granddaughter's body. Yet they treated him as if he was addicted to playing Bingo. I didn't understand it but was nonetheless thrilled that I wouldn't have to play that God-awful adult tickle game anymore. I was happy to know that our family wouldn't split apart as a result of my big secret. Most importantly, I was relieved that the relationship between my grandfather and me wasn't damaged. He just had a problem, or so I was told. He was a "sick man" as my mother and aunts described and he would seek spiritual guidance for a cure.

My mother insisted that I never divulge my secret to my father. She insisted that if I didn't keep my secret from my father, he would kill my grandfather and might go to jail. My mother concerned herself more with withholding the truth from my father, her husband, than what I was going through. She didn't even care enough to ask what her father did to me or if I was okay.

To keep the family from falling apart, I had traded one secret for another. The conversation with my mother led me to view my grandfather as the victim, and I vowed to protect him from my father. I was just happy the abuse was going to stop.

If only it were that simple. My mother and aunts stood idly by for several more years while I was sexually abused at the hands of their father. In the act of ultimate betrayal, my mother continued to let him babysit me. She never expressed an inkling of concern, all while knowing that her first born child, her little girl, was thrust into uncomfortable sexual situations. My life went into a downward spiral of emotions, and my grandfather held the key that I fought for many years to get back in order to free myself.

# CHAPTER FOUR

Contrary to what some may believe child sexual abuse is not always physical. It also includes forms of abuse where physical contact never occurs, such as exposure, voyeurism, and child pornography.

After the night in Lake Almanor, my grandfather, in what I can only assume was his feeble attempt to change, stopped touching my private parts and introduced me to pornographic magazines. I was first abused in this manner, on a day not much different than the rest. By this time my grandparents were my regular babysitters, and usually, I was at their house. My grandmother wasn't home, and I was alone with my grandfather. Being as I thought the abuse had finally stopped; I was once again comfortable in his presence. He never asked me why I told on him; nor did he ever probe to determine exactly what I had shared with my aunt and mother. Because of this, I assumed that the help he was seeking was working. Still, I never completely let my guard down. There was always a nagging feeling that all was not right in the back of my mind. But, I brushed it away and continued to attempt to repair the bond between my grandfather and me. After all, he was my Opa. However, in return, he took advantage of my naivety and vulnerability.

His attempt at noncontact abuse didn't last. Before long he weaseled his way back into my panties. I was watching cartoons, and he called out to me, "Aleesha, come here I want to show you something." I didn't think there was anything suspicious about his request, so I ran to his room, urgently anticipating what he had to show me. Before I told our secret, I would have been skeptical about him calling me into his room, but not this time because my mother and my aunt told me of his promise to stop touching me. They reassured me that he would never touch me again. I blindly believed them because I had no reason to think they would lie to me. They loved me; we were family. So I ran to his room with the energy of a child bursting through the school doors at recess. When I arrived at his room, he asked me to sit on the bed beside him. I did as he said and I flopped beside him like a fish out of water. He slowly got up and shut the door. I thought to myself that it was possibly a new, fun secret that we are about to have; one without the sexual abuse. Yet when he locked the door, I knew whatever he was going to show me wasn't going to be fun. The closed and locked door signified the secret probably involved him touching me away from the gaze of others. The faint click of the turning lock sent chills down my spine, and I began to feel anxious. Bad things always happened after the click.

My grandfather returned to the bed, sat beside me and pulled out a magazine. My nerves began to settle at the sight because I assumed he wanted to read to me. I could never resist a good story time read. The pages rustled softly as he flipped through the magazine in search of a specific page. At first glance it didn't look like any magazine I had ever seen; nevertheless, I gave it my full attention. With each turn of the page, he explained how he came upon the magazine. He said, "I found this magazine in the gutter where your grandmother goes and feeds the stray cats." I nodded as I took in the pages he presented to me. Naked men and women filled the pages. I thought the people in the magazines looked uncomfortable in their funny positions; some were on top of each other. At that time I had not seen a fully naked man and their private parts looked weird to me. However, I gave my grandfather my undivided attention because the magazine seemed to make him happy. Suddenly he stopped flipping the pages. Before me was a picture of a naked woman lying on a bed, with her legs spread wide open, and a man's face buried between them. She wore an expression of pleasure and tightly gripped the man's hair as if she was enjoying herself. I looked up at my grandfather, and he said, "You see this is what people do to each other when they love each other."

I nodded, still unsure why he was showing me the picture. He then said, "If you understand that this is what people do when they love each other, can I do this to you?" My heart stopped. Everything inside me screamed no, but my mouth would not cooperate. I sat quietly unable to speak. He asked again, and I acted as I didn't hear him. My eyes stayed glued to the magazine in hopes that if I sat still long enough, he would lose interest in me. I had no such luck. My grandfather grew inpatient and asked once more. His insistence showed his desperation, and I knew he would not stop asking. I was defeated. I replied, "Okay."

He instructed me to lie back, and I did as I was told. With my eyes pointed up at the ceiling I silently wondered why it was happening to me. Without a logical answer, I gave up and assumed that bending to the will of my grandfather was something that I would have to always do. I became numb, and he had his way with me. He took off my panties, spread my legs and proceeded to do as the man in the magazine. I felt his nose rubbing against me, as he inhaled my scent. The wetness of his tongue against me, made my stomach turn. Vomit rose in my throat, and I forced myself to swallow before it escaped my mouth. It seemed that his head was between my legs for hours. I didn't move the entire time. Fear and anger had frozen me. I wanted to scream at the top of lungs until my voice grew hoarse. My family had lied to me; more specifically my mother had lied to me. I was disappointed that my grandfather let his demons once again control him and frustrated with myself for not being able to say no to him. When he was finished, he looked up at me and asked, "Did you like that? Did that make you feel good?" I was astonished. *Did he just ask me if I liked what he had done to me as if I were a willing participant?* If I had been able to find my voice, I would have let him know that it repulsed me. However, since he, in the words of my mother, had a problem, I had no choice but to submit to his needs until he could be healed by the Bible my aunt had given him.

He repeated his previous questions and broke me from my thoughts. I answered him with a quietly mumbled, "Yes." Satisfied with my answer, my grandfather lifted himself off of me. I quickly hopped off of the bed and put on my panties before he unlocked the bedroom door. As I crossed the threshold of the room, he reminded me that what went on between us was a secret. Other than his reminder we never spoke of what happened again and went about our day as if it never occurred.

Each time he and grandmother babysat me, my grandfather's actions progressed. His fingers grew increasingly comfortable on my body, particularly with my vagina. He began to explore my insides and slowly destroyed what innocence I had left. Whenever his hand or face was between my legs, I would close my eyes and think of being in a better place. No matter how hard I tried to remember that he had a problem, I still felt like I was being punished. As time passed, my grandfather grew restless with using his fingers. They were no longer able to satisfy his twisted desires, and he graduated to using his penis.

The first time it happened, he sickeningly and sweetly asked me to lie on my back across the bed. As I complied, he lovingly assured me that everything was going to be okay. I knew that I would be anything but, as he tugged at my cartoon embroidered underwear. I closed my eyes to avoid the sight of his partially naked body after I heard the familiar sound of pants unzipping. "Ouch Opa," I cried when he attempted to force himself inside of me. Though not from a lack of trying, having sexual intercourse with his seven-year-old grandchild did not bring about the climax he was expecting. So he stopped, and he satisfied his urges with his usual rubbing and touching.

I started to just come to grips with knowing and understanding that this is my life. I use to think to myself that this has to be normal maybe my uncomfortable feeling was just due to the unfamiliarity of the situation.

Just as I had on previous occasions, I went about my day as if nothing had happened. What choice did I have? Telling my family was pointless. I had done that, to no avail.; and absolutely nothing had changed. They smoothed over their father's actions to cater to his feelings at the expense of the physical and emotional pain I was enduring. Without anyone to protect me, I did the only thing I could. I waited and prayed for the Lord to heal him. Needless to say, the guidance my aunt spoke of never came. He continued to molest me. As time went on, he brazenly worried less about getting caught; probably because I had already told, and nothing had happened to him. It was now understood, that what went on between us was a secret; he no longer reminded me. My grandfather would have his way with me without so much as a second thought to how wrong it was. I was alone, and my grandfather knew it.

Once he introduced pornographic magazines into his demented repertoire, he always kept them hidden in plain sight amongst his golfing magazines. He did this because he knew I would be curious and peek at them from time to time. Unbeknownst to me, it was all a part of his sinister plan to keep my mind sexualized. Not to mention he was hell-bent on reenacting the images that filled the pages.

As a child the male genitalia grossed me out; therefore, when my grandfather asked me to touch his penis, I said no without hesitation. He stripped naked, as we stood together in the bathroom as if by seeing it would persuade me to go against my better judgment. I shook my head vigorously from left to right indicating that I was sticking to my answer. Seeing that I was not inclined to change my mind, he came up with what he thought was the perfect solution to my squeamishness. He walked out of the bathroom, only to return with a plastic shopping bag. Still naked, he positioned himself with one leg propped up on the edge of the bathroom sink, covered his penis with the bag, and motioned for me to come to him. Without a hint of irony, he told me that I could touch him being as there would not be any skin to skin contact between my hand and his penis. His reassuring tone convinced me that there was logic in his words and after his third time asking me, I agreed to his quiet plea. I was unsure of what to do. However, my grandfather was all too happy to assist me until I was able to please him on my own. I was caught by surprise when the bag filled with an explosion of warm fluid. Grateful that my part appeared to be over, I waited for further instructions. But I was only met with silence before he walked out of the bathroom like nothing happened. I eventually left the bathroom, happy to be able to return to playing.

Life never allowed me to be a child. My grandfather stole any chance at ever having a normal childhood. The line between love and abuse became indistinguishable, and my behavior and beliefs began to reflect the damage inflicted upon me. I started to believe that other grandfathers did to their grandchildren, what mine did to me. My Barbie dolls took the brunt of abuse from my overly sexualized mind. Even though I hated the things my grandfather did to me, I insisted it was normal. I used my grandfather's example as how to treat them. I pressed their naked, plastic bodies against one another and licked their breast.

It wasn't long before, I exhibited sexual behavior towards other children. Together, a male classmate and I would escape behind a school building to pull up our shirts and rub our bodies together. School became a problem for me or more like I was a problem for the school. I was kicked out of numerous elementary schools due to my unpredictable behavior. My relationship with my grandfather confused me. Without anyone to offer the clarity I desperately needed, my confusion manifested as anger, which I then took out on my schoolmates. Despite the fact that I was somewhat shy, my behavior was loud, boisterous, and often just too much. I regularly spoke out of turn and disrupted the class. I even went so far as to become the class clown to mask the pain I felt.

Ultimately my behavior raised serious concerns with the school administration. They reached their breaking point when I pushed over a bookshelf with the intention of it landing on a sleeping infant. It was only by the grace of God that someone was able to catch it and push it away from the baby. My teachers were at a loss. They didn't understand why I behaved as I did, nor did they care to find out. Honestly, I didn't know why I did the things I did. All I knew was that I didn't know how to put my feelings into words. I couldn't articulate my pain and remained fearful that whenever I was able to find them no one would listen or take the time to help me.

I thought I had been saved, the day the social worker showed up on our doorstep. My mother greeted her at the door with a look of uncertainty as to why she was there. The social worker shared that she was employed by child protective services, the government agency that responds to reports of child abuse or neglect. She then asked if she could come in to discuss the reason for her visit. When I heard this, I thought someone would finally be able to stop my grandfather; however, the social worker's visit had nothing to do with Opa.

Once inside, the social worker began to explain that she was there because the gash across my check had been brought to her attention. My mother knew exactly the gash to which she was referring. It was the result of a simple mistake; still, it did not erase the look of worry on her face. She unknowingly and accidentally grazed my cheek with her ring when she reprimanded me for throwing dirt into my cousin's face while we played. She didn't have a chance to say much before my father overheard and intervened. He was a quiet, comical man but was not to be taken lightly. He told the social worker exactly how I mistakenly received the gash and invited her to leave his home if she didn't like the way his children were disciplined. Considering she recognized the gash was an accident and not a case of abuse, the social worker took my father up on his offer and left.

# CHAPTER FIVE

*A child who is the victim of prolonged sexual abuse usually develops low self-esteem, a feeling of worthlessness and an abnormal or distorted view of sex.*

I was the living embodiment of the above statement at nine- years-old. I was not mentally prepared for the repeated sexual abuse perpetrated upon me. Honestly, I don't think anyone ever is. To cope, I learned to submit to what was happening to me, and slowly I adapted. Daydreams played themselves out in my head while my grandfather had his way with my body. It was the only way to protect myself. My family had proven that they had no interest in helping me. I began to believe they knew the abuse continued but didn't care. There was no other reason why my mother would constantly leave me alone with my grandfather.

He was a rich man. And although I was young, I knew that if my mother sent him to jail, her lifestyle would drastically change. The influx of money and the perks that came along with it would be no more. To me, that seemed to be more important to her than me. This thought raced through my mind from time to time, when I had a free moment to think. But I continued life as if nothing was happening and carried on the best way I knew how. As crazy as it may sound, I was never angry at my family because I looked at them as the victims. They had to live with the fact that they had a sick father who was unable to control himself. So in my mind, by staying quiet, I was protecting them all, including my grandfather; which allowed them to live normal lives.

Family vacations were frequent and were a regular part of our lives. As a family, we loved beaches. We enjoyed the feeling of the sand against our feet and taking in scenic views that only the beach could offer. There was a freedom I didn't often know, in standing in the wet sand as the waves washed over my feet and quickly retreated into the massive ocean. For however brief a moment, I didn't have any other cares in the world. But just as the waves never stopped rolling, my reality was ever-present.

During one of our family beach trips, the day began as it would for any family without a pedophile for its patriarch. We talked, laughed and ate mini sandwiches, while sitting shoeless in the sand. We had everything we needed to make the most of our time on the beach. There was even a tent if anyone wanted to shield themselves from the sun or relax away from the sand. It was my mother's green and white dome tent, and fit three comfortably. Whereas it was everyone else's peaceful respite, for me, it would play a part in a beach day I would forever try to forget.

While everyone went for a walk on the beach, I stayed behind in the tent. I sat inside nibbling on a piece of chicken and sipping on a Diet Coke. I didn't think much of being alone until I realized that I wasn't. In the middle of eating it struck me that everyone was gone, except for my grandfather. I peeked out of the tent to survey the beach, hoping that another family member, any family member, decided not to partake in a spontaneous walk along the beach.

To no surprise, my grandfather was the only person I saw. He entered the tent and closed the zippered door behind him leaving it open just enough to be able to see the family's return. He was silent. There were no words spoken as he positioned himself behind me. Past experience dictated exactly what was about to happen; I didn't need instruction. I put my Diet Coke down; then the chicken bone and waited to follow his lead. He pushed my hair to the side and unbuckled my denim overalls. With one eye focused on the peephole and the familiarity he had come to develop, he found the parts of my body that excited him most. My thoughts immediately escaped to a better place, as he took control of my body. It's how I maintained my sanity. If I weren't present, it wasn't real. All I had to do was occupy my thoughts long enough for it to all be over.

Regardless of how far my thoughts traveled outside of the tent, I could not stop wondering why everyone had left me. Why hadn't they taken me with them on the walk? Why was I excluded? The shift in my grandfather's weight broke me from my thoughts. He had gotten all he needed from me. Before leaving the tent, he peeked through the peephole to make we were still alone, wiped his hands and exited out of the tent.

I sat in silence, as I buckled my overalls making sure to leave one strap dangling to look exactly as I had before the family left. I sipped my Diet Coke, and I waited for the ruined beach day to be over. It puzzled me how he could do what he did me, and then, as it never happened, go back to his life. He didn't appear to be bothered at all. He could look his daughters and wife in the face with an expression of joy, knowing that it was his perversion with his nine-year-old granddaughter that put his smile there. With me, he was one person, and it seemed he was someone totally different with everyone else. He was the exemplification of Dr. Jekyll and Mr. Hyde. In spite of the abuse I suffered at his hands, it was hard for me to hate him. I struggled with knowing who he was behind closed doors and witnessing the caring and selfless man he appeared to be at all other times.

The years of sexual and mental abuse began to take its toll on my wellbeing. I began to feel worthless, and my self-confidence was all but non-existent. It was increasingly harder to maintain any semblance of normalcy. I became uncomfortable with myself and my body. I was a child, who was at the sexual whim of her grandfather.

Around the age of eleven or twelve, he picked me up from school and tried to convince me to orally copulate him. I ignored him, in the hopes that he would eventually stop asking. I had no such luck. He wasn't fazed as I turned a deaf ear. In fact, it seemed to encourage him as evidenced by the erotic things he said to me.

I continued to sit in silence as he drove to Baskin-Robbins, where he ordered a strawberry shake topped with whip cream for himself and a vanilla ice cream cone for me. From the corner of my eye, I could see him ravenously watching me lick my ice cream. I ignored him still, as he parked in one of Baskin-Robbins' more isolated parking spaces. I said nothing as he unzipped his pants, exposed his penis, and covered himself with whipped cream. His desperate pleas for me to orally satisfy him hung in the air. I was unmoved. My eyes stayed fixated on any and everything outside that window, refusing to look in his direction. I had no doubt that if I did, I would once again feel sorry for him. In the beginning, I always felt sorry for him and martyred myself while I waited for God to heal him. However, as I grew older, it became more and more apparent my aunt's Bible was not working.

He wasn't forceful in his assault, he never was. Instead, my grandfather was a cunning and calculated predator. He used a silver tongue and guilt to carry out his misdeeds. On this occasion, his smooth talk failed him, leaving him no choice but to not press the issue further. He pulled out of the Baskin-Robbins' parking lot and drove us to his house for the weekend; in silence.

Once inside, the events of the day replayed, and it dawned on me that if I ignored my grandfather's sexual requests, he would stop asking. I found very little power in this new revelation, considering all my grandfather had put me through. I was alone, both in life and in my room. My reflection innocently stared back at me from my mirrored closet doors, and all I saw was my pain. It wasn't fair. All of the heartache and agony I felt rushed out of me. I screamed and cursed God, "Why do I have to have such a messed up life?" There was no one to answer. I knew there wouldn't be, but still, I repeated my question over and over. Each time asked my despair became increasingly apparent. I was furious. Why was I the one suffering while the rest of my family went about their normal, happy lives? Why did I have to consider my grandfather's feelings when he, nor anyone else, cared about mine? I no longer cared that he was sick. Unfortunately, whether I cared or not, my grandfather continued to use me as he wished.

Somewhere along the line, my grandfather began to touch me less and derive more sexual pleasure from verbally assaulting me and exposing himself. From my vantage point, it seemed that he especially liked to reveal himself aboard his boat. Whenever the family gathered on his private boat, he always found some way to corner me and expose his hidden jewels. He was keenly aware that my mother and others usually gravitated toward the front of the boat, while as I typically avoided the adult fun by hanging out in the back. Once he knew I was alone, he would position himself with his back facing the other adults to prevent them from seeing his disgusting behavior; which always went unnoticed. My grandfather had his positioning down to a science. He would elevate himself on any given object, making him stand significantly taller than me. After he was sure his crotch was directly in my line of sight, he would call my name then wave and point to his bared penis. It was not lost on me that he never wore underwear during these times. The lack of undergarments made it obvious to me that his behavior was premeditated. The smirk he wore on his face indicated that it was deliberate. He intended to get a reaction out of me. The more shock or disgust I showed, the more excited he became. Over time, I learned not to give him the satisfaction of reacting, so he would move along, and I could enjoy the serenity of the ocean without interruption.

As I grew older, my grandfather's perverse infatuation with me could no longer be satisfied with his proclivities of the past. He wanted my body in its entirety. He wanted sexual intercourse. After his failed attempt when I was younger, my grandfather made no secret of his plans for me when I turned eighteen.

Eventually following my aunt's lead, my grandparents moved to Texas, which granted me a reprieve from his constant abuse. Though I was not totally free of him, there were extended periods of time during which I did not have to endure his sexual advances. On one occasion when my family was visiting my grandparents, my brother Jayson and I were innocently separated from my mother on a ride to my aunt's house after dinner. Jayson, who was seven or eight at the time, and I had the unfortunate luck of riding with my grandfather.

Considering that it was a short car ride to my aunt's, coupled with the fact that I wasn't alone, I didn't foresee having any problems. However, my grandfather was never one to be swayed. Suddenly, he began speaking to me in Dutch. I wasn't fluent in the language, but I was able to identify two words, my name and the number eighteen. He asked me if I understood what he said, to which I replied no. Without warning or hesitation, he repeated his statement in English and said, "Remember, you said when you turn eighteen that you would have sex with me." My skin tingled with embarrassment. I couldn't believe that he had the gall to say that in front of my younger brother. Words escaped me, but I did manage to reply, "uh huh, yeah," with the hope that it would deter him from continuing the inappropriate conversation. It was my only recourse. Again, he had forced me into a situation that reminded me how depressing my life was.

I rested my head on the back of the front seat and thought back to a much simpler time, long ago, when I wasn't my grandfather's obsession. Although I knew it was impossible, I wished for the ability to rewind my life back to when I was pure; a time before my grandfather had defiled me.

# CHAPTER SIX

A child who is the victim of prolonged sexual abuse usually develops low self-esteem, a feeling of worthlessness and an abnormal or distorted view of sex. The child may become withdrawn and mistrustful of adults.

My time in middle school seemed to fly by, even though I suffered from low self-esteem, and feelings of worthlessness. In my attempt to feel normal, I occupied myself with school activities. Basketball was one of my favorites. I wasn't that good of a player, but I had more control of the game than I did my life. The challenge of trying to get the ball in the net fulfilled me. On the court, I found just enough of a distraction to drown out my home life. It was almost as if I were someone else on the hardwood floor. Whereas I was socially awkward elsewhere, during practice and games I danced, smiled and had fun. As soon as I walked off the court, I returned to my withdrawn, shy and insecure self. To put it mildly, I never felt good enough for anyone.

During school, I would let other students push me around. Despite my relatively tall height, I was an easy target. Truthfully, I was scared; mostly to be myself because I didn't know who I was. I couldn't expect those around me to know who Aleesha really was when middle school Aleesha didn't exist. I hadn't grown past the day before my grandfather first touched me.

To no fault of their own, the few friends I had knew nothing about my horrible life outside of school. Nor did they know how depressed I was. I kept it from them. It was a dirty secret that I held close to me so they wouldn't think that I was as messed up as I really was. It never occurred to them why I dressed differently than they did. They could have never imagined why I always covered my body and refused to wear tight or revealing clothes. I'm sure they assumed it was only a fashion choice; oh, how I wished it were.

There was one good friend that I had who just so happened to be a boy. With us both being biracial, we clicked immediately based on our similarity; we understood each other. The two of us were so close that my mother and father let me spend nights over at his house. They weren't worried about us getting into trouble and never saw him as a threat. Somehow they knew that our time together was innocent. Whenever my friend and I were together, we laughed, played games and told each other everything. Well, almost everything. I could never bring myself to share what I was going through with my grandfather.

We had so much in common it was uncanny. I wouldn't find out until years, after we both found our voices and unyielding strength, that our bond was one of hidden pain and resiliency. Unbeknownst to the other at the time, we both had secrets that we were sworn to never talk about. But until that day came, that we were no longer prisoners to our truths, we navigated middle and high school with painted smiles to stay off of the radar.

My days in middle school soon passed. I left B. Gale Wilson Elementary and headed for ninth grade at Sem Yeto High. Just as I was leaving one school for a new beginning, I hoped that I would also be able to leave behind all of the bad memories held in those years. With a little bit of soul-searching, I resigned to finally allow myself to break free of the shell of a person I was. By that time, my grandfather had all but stopped with the physical sexual abuse and the occurrences of verbal abuse or exposing himself only happened every now and then. The worst was behind me, and my goal became learning how to live with what had been done to me, the best way I knew how.

Old habits die hard, and at the beginning of high school, I behaved as I knew best; timid and withdrawn. By the time I reached tenth grade, I had reverted to the rebellious nature I once possessed in elementary school. When I was quiet and reserved, no one asked any questions. No one seemed to try and understand what brewed beneath the surface. On the other hand, when I was rebellious people asked questions; people paid attention. So I gave them something to look at; something they could talk about and maybe eventually ask the right questions.

I became the jokester, the class clown. I was the student whose seat was incessantly moved to the back of the class, away from others, in an attempt to control my disruptive behavior. My teachers always sent letters home, and I never received a report card that didn't note that I was disruptive and too talkative. Though I wasn't a model student, my teachers never failed to also point out that I was a natural born leader, endowed with the ability to influence others for the better or worst. At the time, I didn't fully grasp what they meant. So instead of becoming the leader they thought I was, I continued to follow others, most often down the wrong path.

My friends and I were at the age where boys became almost a singular focus; at least to them. I didn't have the same feelings. That's not to say that there weren't boys that I liked; of course, there were. But just looking at a boy directly in his eyes for an extended period of time scared me. So much so, that I would have to look away. I feared they would see that which I tried fiercely to hide. I didn't want to be judged or seen as dirty because of the things my grandfather did to me.

If I were lucky enough to find a boy who liked me enough to overlook the fact that I never really looked at him and still wanted to be my boyfriend, our relationship only lasted a matter of days. Regardless of how much I liked him, I wasn't able to show the affection to match my feelings. Simplest gestures of affection terrified me. I could barely handle innocent hugging, therefore when a boyfriend wanted a kiss, I would lose myself in terror.

I hadn't attempted to kiss a boy since my first try in the seventh grade. To say it was traumatizing is a grand understatement. Two of my girlfriends were on a date at the movie theater with their respective boyfriends, while I tagged along to keep the guy's third wheel company. My friends sat on their boyfriend's laps and counted down coordinated kissing. When they reached one, the two couples began making out. I looked on, slightly disgusted and yet intrigued. Though I didn't show it, it upset me that I was too shy and unsure of myself to do such a simple thing. As if on cue, both couples' eyes locked on me when they broke from their passionate kissing. Their gazes burned through me and questioned why I was not kissing my date as planned. They teasingly scolded me, and threw popcorn while they chanted in unison, "You're not going to kiss him." I felt like an outcast and had to escape their mocking. I jumped out of my seat, ran through the darkened theater, and made a beeline to the bathroom; which was where I stayed until my mother picked me up.

The experience was so horrifying that it paralyzed me with fright anytime I thought about kissing another boy. To make matters worse, I was in high school, and I knew that once boys stepped on first base, it wouldn't be long before they were ready for a home run.

Despite all of this, I nonetheless attempted to kiss a boy again. I wanted to show my then boyfriend that I cared for him. Much like my first attempt, my boyfriend and I weren't alone; we were in my friend's backyard surrounded by others. I willed it to be better than the last time and repeated silently to myself: *Don't embarrass yourself this time.* I closed my eyes, and our heads slowly moved toward each other, but our lips never touched. I bolted from my seat and ran away from my boyfriend as fast as I could. I ended up hiding under a bush, where I stayed for about thirty to forty-five minutes until I built up the courage to poke my head out to make sure the search had been called off. When it was clear that my friends were no longer looking for me, I ran to the nearest pay phone and called my mother to pick me up.

Notwithstanding all of my failed attempts at kissing, I eventually had my first real kiss. Because there was always such quick turnaround time between boyfriends, it wasn't until boyfriend number four that I was able to follow through. It was probably because he was very persistent that if I liked him, I would kiss him. I finally gave in. My rebellious nature was in full-force at the time; therefore, I had no problem skipping school to hang out with him.

On one such day, my cousin Jennifer and I invited our boyfriends over to her house. Upon their arrival, she and I retreated to separate bedrooms with our significant others. I, like always, froze and was unable, or maybe even unwilling, to shake the nerves. My boyfriend had no compassion toward my fears. He looked me in my eyes and said, "If you don't kiss me, it's over." His words hurt. They were sharp and could have only hurt worse if they were made of blades. I didn't want to lose another boyfriend. I couldn't lose another boyfriend. I acquiesced, inhaled deeply and asked him to turn off the lights. He did as I asked. I put the covers over my head and followed his lead since I wasn't as experienced with kissing as he was. Admittedly, I had difficulty at first, but once I got the gist of it, we kissed for what seemed like hours. It wasn't as bad as I had imaged it to be. More so, it was nice to experience a real kiss; one that I could use to replace the thoughts of the disgraceful sexual things done with my grandfather. When the kissing was over, and our eyes met, I noticed that he had the same satisfied look in his eyes as my grandfather after he had his way with me. It then occurred to me, that men saw my body as a tool to satisfy their sexual urges. I started to understand that if I wanted boys to like me, then I would have to show my affection with sexual acts. This realization, never led me to become promiscuous, but it did play a large role in me never knowing my worth or the worth of my body.

The pressures of dating, coupled with coping with past abuse led me to be increasingly rebellious and unruly. My entire childhood, including my teenage years, was filled with acts of defiance. But I transformed into an all-out hell raiser in tenth and eleventh grades. In those two years alone I was suspended from school approximately ten times. The things I did were stupid and for no other reason than attention-grabbing. For instance, my friend and I once stole a box of chicken that a student brought in to share with the class. When we were sure no one was looking, I took the chicken, raced to the nearest secluded area on campus, and devoured the entire box. Three hours later we decided to return to class, only to walk into a search party on the hunt to find us. The principal, teachers, and students were all looking for us. Once we were discovered to be the chicken bandits, my friend and I were suspended.

Another incident that landed the two of us in the principal's office, and on the verge of yet another suspension, was the time we threw nachos onto students and faculty from a balcony above while they ate lunch. We attempted to run off, but in the end, we were caught and faced our usual punishment.

Little by little I was losing self-control. The thought of me ever being a model student or normal seemed like a distant memory. I began to believe that I was destined to always be a messed up person. On top of that, I was certain that no one would ever delve deeper to determine why I was acting out. Being the case, I figured if no one else cared then there was no reason to change and I focused my attention on my new interest, boys.

The opposite sex became my driving force, and I was soon smitten with a boy that lived the next city over in Vallejo. Vallejo was located in the North Bay region of San Francisco, which was only a fifteen-minute ride from Fairfield. The slight distance made it easy for us to see each other. I would attend his school's basketball games and other city events just to be close to him. Every Saturday I made it a point to visit him and eventually, the dedication that I put into our friendship paid off as I hoped. He asked me to be his girlfriend.

Although we stayed relatively close to each other, I still needed my mother's assistance to visit him. Each time we met, she would drop me off and then come back to pick me up. There were often times that my mother didn't want to make the trip, but she gave in once I fussed enough. However, there was on time that she absolutely refused to take me. Regardless of how much I pleaded and argued, she didn't budge. Naturally, this angered me, and with each no I grew progressively irritated. I didn't want to disappoint my boyfriend by canceling our date to the movies. Being as I was reduced to believing that my value was only found in my body, I felt that my time and our smooching sessions were all I was able to offer him. I was still a virgin; however, I still held a sense of obligation to give him some part of me. And I couldn't let my mother stand in my way.

After she told me no for the hundredth time, I stomped to my room with fury in my heart and tears in my eyes. With each passing second, I grew angrier and angrier. I couldn't believe she wouldn't do something as simple as taking me to my boyfriend's house when upon her insistence, I protected her perverted father for years. I was pissed and was unable to shake the feeling. If she weren't going to say yes because it was the right thing to do, at least in my mind; then I would have to make her say it. I decided right then and there, I would blackmail her. Fueled by my brilliant idea, I returned to her and presented my request in a new fashion. I said to her, "If you don't take me to Vallejo, I'm telling my dad that Opa molested me." Her eyes widened, and her face drained of any color. I knew I had her, her silence spoke volumes. She stood from her seat, grabbed her car keys, and headed to the car. With a smirk on my face, I quickly gathered my things and followed behind as I waited to be shepherded to Vallejo.

My victory that day was hollow, and the joy I felt from being victorious was short-lived. Although I got what I wanted, I didn't feel good about how I got it. I wasn't that type of person. However, that did not sway me. Keeping my abuse a secret was eating me alive, so if I could use it to my advantage to restore some of the happiness my grandfather had stolen, then so be it. My mother continued to take me across town whenever I wanted, and when she didn't want to, I reminded her of my threat. Like anyone with so much to lose, she would fall into place and take me where I needed to go. The shoe was now on the other foot. There was someone else who had to deal with the pain my grandfather caused. Deep down, I hated that it had to be that way. Ultimately, I stopped using my grandfather's sins against my mother. After all, she wasn't the person that molested me. So I turned my focus to the person who deserved to be blackmailed; my sick pedophile of a grandfather.

One day, I walked up to my mother and announced that I wanted a car. Before she could open her mouth to tell me what I assumed would have been no, I told her to call my grandfather. My message to him was clear: if he didn't send the money to buy me a car, I was going to tell my father what he had done to me. My mother wasted no time doing exactly as I had instructed. She returned from the call with the news that my grandfather agreed to send me one thousand dollars, under one condition that I would never ever contact him again with any future undertakings of blackmail. I agreed to his terms. At sixteen-years-old, I naively believed that one thousand dollars was a lot of money and I had endless options. But

I was wrong; I was only able to afford a '86 Toyota Corolla. I was crestfallen. Everything he had put me through, everything he did to me, all the pain, hurt and trauma, was worth only a thousand dollars to him. The worst part was that I gave into it and also believed that was all I was worth.

Irrespective of the guilt I hung onto from hurting my mother and blackmailing my grandfather, I carried on with my life. I still had my car, and all was right in my world until a faithful incident that brought me back to the pain that was ceaselessly in my life.

In 2003, I was in the school office with my friend and often partner in crime. Apart from the two of us, the office was empty. Never one to let an opportunity go by, my friend pulled a black marker from his bag and wrote the word "bitch" across the name plaque mounted outside the principal's door. After admiring his handiwork, he noticed the marker he used was washable. That simply would not have done the job he wanted it to. He reached back into his bag and retrieved a permanent marker. Instead of rewriting the word himself, he passed the marker to me.

Just as I was about to write the first letter, I heard the secretary yell out, "Aleesha, what are you doing?!" My first instinct was to run back to my classroom and sit at my desk as if nothing ever happened. As I tried to go unnoticed, I silently prayed that it would all go away. Of course, it didn't. The sound of my name over the intercom along with instructions to report to the principal's office immediately let me know that I would have no such luck. I was summarily suspended, the only difference being that on this occasion the school called the police because I had committed an act of vandalism.

Upon their arrival, the police officers walked over to me and placed handcuffs around my wrist. The tears began to immediately flow. I was only 16-years-old, a fact that they didn't seem to care about one bit. Meanwhile, the principal had called my mother. She was informed of my wrongdoings and asked to come pick me up. She was in the office, not even a second and I could tell that she was furious with me. I lifted my head, which had been lowered in shame, looked her in her eyes and said, "Mom help!"

Her rebuttal was unexpected. She said, "Nope let the police take you to jail for whatever you did." I couldn't believe my ears. There was no way she would let them take me to jail. Not me, her own daughter. The same one who kept her family's secret shame. Adding insult to injury, one of the police officers laughed at her response or more like he laughed at me. Still the handcuffs were removed, and my mother was given specific instructions to take me to the Fairfield Police Station to fill out paperwork regarding the incident. My mother did as she was told and we drove in silence to the Fairfield Police Station.

Once we were at the police station, my mother and I were separated. She stayed in the lobby and filled out paperwork, while another officer escorted me to a tiny back room. I was incredibly nervous. The confined space looked like an interrogation room right off the set of *Law & Order*. The resemblance made my thoughts run wild, as I pondered my fate. I didn't know if I was going to jail, or if my mother would have to pay a fine. I didn't know if I was going to have to do community service and pick up trash on the side of the street while I faced the embarrassment of my friends laughing at me. Then it occurred to me how angry this would make my father. Like my mother, he was fed up with my constant bad behavior.

In the midst of my thoughts, the officer closed the door behind him, sat down and began questioning me. In the beginning, the questions were innocent enough and expected all things considered. He asked where I lived, my age and the details of the day's events outside the principal's office. His questions soon took a turn. The officer inquired about my childhood, and then, as if he had posed the question a million times, he asked if I had ever been molested. The question caught me off guard, and I paused. I could not look away from him, I was in awe. Did he know? Of all the questions he could have asked pertaining to my act of vandalism, why had he chosen to ask me that particular question? I thought to myself that I finally had another chance to say something.

The officer's one question gave me hope that my grandfather would once and for all be punished and I, in turn, would be able to begin to heal.

I responded to the officer with a simple, "Yes," before going on to disclose the sordid details of my molestation at the hands of my grandfather. The dam had been broken. Years of pent-up frustration and secrets spilled from me. The officer intently listened to all I had to say. When I was finished, he questioned whether or not my grandfather currently lived around any children that he could possibly be molesting. I let him know that he and my grandmother lived in Texas, just the two of them with no children around. He quickly scrawled notes in his pad before retracting his pen and muffling the words, "I'll be right back." With that, he quietly walked out of the room. He was gone for only a brief moment before he returned with my mother in tow. For as many thoughts that ran through my head just a few moments ago, the only thing I could think at that moment was *Oh crap.* I just spilled the family secret and instead of telling my father or any other family member; I told a police officer to the potential detriment of my family. There was nothing I could do about it at that point, other than to sit back and watch everything unfold. What was done was done.

My mother took the seat next to me; with the assumption that her being there was just another part of my vandalism charge. The officer once again closed the door and took his seat. I sat with bated breath as a momentary hush surrounded the three of us. I turned to my mother wearing the same remorseful eyes I had in the principal's office and softly said, "Mom I'm sorry, but I told." She looked at me, her eyes full of questions, and then directed her glare at the officer before turning back to me.

"You told what?" she asked. Her face was fixed in an expression of uncertainty.

Before I lost my courage, I responded, "I told the police officer that Opa molested me when I was younger."

With no other choice, my mother reluctantly admitted that I was, indeed, molested by her father. She explained that I had come to her when I was younger and shared that Opa was touching me, but she and her sisters had confronted him, and he had stopped. As to make things better, she informed the officer that he now lived in Texas, away from other children, so he wasn't molesting anyone any longer.

Undeterred by my mother's attempt to persuade him that everything was under control, the officer still requested my grandfather's phone number. He wanted to confirm both of our stories, in addition to substantiating that he wasn't around any children. There must have been something in his tone that let my mother know that his request would not go unheard. Therefore, she complied and gave him all of the pertinent information.

The car ride home was uncomfortable. Neither my mother nor I said a word. The fear of the unknown haunted me, and I began to wonder what would become of my actions. Would I be punished for spilling family secrets? The thought made me cringe? The only thing that troubled me more was how and what my mother was going to tell my father about what happened at the police station. She had successfully kept him in the dark for years; would she now tell him everything? Or would she sanitize the day to make it more palatable to him and absolve her of any guilt? She did exactly as I expected; she told him everything making sure to exclude the molestation. None the wiser, my father handed down a punishment befitting my vandalism; while I drowned in frustration and my mother's betrayal.

That night, I contemplated disclosing the absolute truth to my father, but I couldn't. For all the strength I had at the police station, I sat paralyzed by the possibility of telling him. My resolve was gone. I kept my thoughts captive, held them hostage in my mind where they only hurt me.

The next day, my mother asked that we have a conversation regarding the events of the previous day. Albeit more of a demand than a request, I complied with her invitation to talk. I was all ears; I couldn't wait to hear what she had to say. Nothing could have prepared me for what I heard. She let me know that she reached out to my grandfather to warn him that the Fairfield

Police Department would be contacting him with respect to the statement I made. Before delving into the conversation, she asked her father to step outside to prevent my grandmother from overhearing the exchange. Through all of the years, I was sexually abused, there were two people my family made a concerted effort to hide the facts from, my father and my grandmother. By maintaining discretion while she and my grandfather spoke, my mother tried her best to keep it that way. However, my grandmother's suspicions were raised by the need for privacy between her husband and daughter.

At the conclusion of the phone call, my grandmother questioned why she wasn't privy to the conversation. Taken off guard by the inquiry, he hid a little truth in a lie. He told her that he had exposed himself to me once when I was a child. And I had blackmailed him into getting me a car with the information. Resultantly, a detective was going to contact him soon.

My mother went on to say that my grandmother called her back immediately with the news that my grandfather was contemplating suicide if he had to go to jail. She followed by saying that if he did, she would kill herself as well. As I listened to my mother, I waited patiently for her to tell me that my grandfather apologized for his actions or at the very least showed some type of remorse. Furthermore, I fully anticipated her telling me how upset my grandmother was that her husband would do such things to her darling granddaughter. I was on the edge of my seat waiting for my mother to discuss my grandmother's concern for me, but I waited in vain. No such words were spoken. My grandfather never apologized, and my grandmother never sought to comfort me. My grandmother's only concern was her husband. It was impossible for her to care less about my feelings or wellbeing. The woman I had known to be a loving and thoughtful grandmother was gone and in her place was a coldhearted, selfish woman whose sole objective was protecting her pedophile of a husband, not the child he abused.

It was frightening to hear that they were choosing suicide as a way out, and old feelings of guilt resurfaced. I wouldn't know what to do if they killed themselves because of me, so as always I felt obligated to put his feelings before mine. I vowed to keep my mouth shut and continue living a lie because my truth created too much chaos. If my grandfather was one thing, he was consistent. He once again painted himself as the victim and I, in turn, felt like the transgressor.

To make matters worse, a few days later my mother mentioned that the detective got around to speaking with my grandfather. As expected he asked his questions, however, thanks to my mother's preparation, my grandfather answered him coolly, calmly and seemingly logically. And just like that, the thought of someone coming to my rescue dissipated like vapor in the wind.

For the second time, I told someone who I believed would protect me and nothing happened.

We never discussed the issue again, and I was left to assume that his lies were more believable than my truth. Or maybe it was because I waited too long to say something. Either way, no one gave any indication that they cared about my past. Dejected, I crawled back into my shell to shield myself from the outside world.

# CHAPTER SEVEN

*Children can recover from sexual abuse and go on to live good fulfilled lives. The best predictor of their recovery is support and love from their main caregiver.*

Growing up, my two primary caregivers were my mother and father. My father was unaware of me being sexually abused, and my mother encouraged me to stay silent. Not only that, but she also failed to do anything to make my situation any better. Therefore, it goes without saying that I lacked the support needed to recover from the trauma I suffered. I did as much as I could on my own, but my efforts left me frustrated and feeling that no one would ever understand my pain. That is until one night, I got help from the last place I expected; television.

I was eating dinner, or at least I was supposed to be. However, I was actually doing more daydreaming than eating. The television played in the background, but I wasn't watching it. It was on more so to fill the room with noise. Then something caught my attention. It was VH1's *Behind the Music* featuring Missy Elliot. Her voice broke through my thoughts, and I heard her say that as a child she was molested by a family member. Hearing that, I turned and gave the television my full undivided attention.

I couldn't believe that Miss Elliot had been through the same thing I had. I looked at her in a new light and at once developed genuine respect for her. I was awestruck, as I listened to her recount her abuse on national television in front of millions of viewers. Her strength and openness were inspiring, and I began to feel silly about withholding the truth of my abuse from my father. Even though my aunts, my mother, and even the police knew; my father, the main person who should have known, didn't.

Missy's episode of *Behind the Music* enlightened me beyond measure. Whereas I thought I was alone in the world, I now had proof that the type of abuse I suffered wasn't just happening to me. It wasn't that I found joy in knowing others suffered my fate because I wouldn't wish it upon anyone. But what it did was open my mind to the possibilities. Up until that point, I was my only resource in my healing. What I didn't know how to fix, was left broken. However, if others shared my pain, there was hope for me. I could divert my attention from negative past experiences and focus on anything positive that I could find.

In 2004, my grandfather went in for a routine checkup; however, the visit ended up being anything but routine. After a thorough examination, his doctor diagnosed him with cryptogenic fibrosing alveolitis, a rare lung disease with high morbidity and mortality rates. There wasn't a cure for it at the time, but there was a drug being tested at a facility in Texas. If my grandfather chose to, he could check himself into the facility and receive the experimental drug. The one drawback was the facility was very costly, and he did not want to pay the expense. Therefore, he declined the care they offered.

I was saddened when I first found out about his illness; however, I also felt inexplicable joy and happiness. It's hard to explain because it's terrible to find contentment in someone else's misfortune. But, regardless of his health, I remained furious with him because of everything he did to me as a child. I rationalized that his illness was God's way of punishing him; when so many earthly beings simply let him have his way with me. There was an internal battle brewing within me, and I often questioned my unspeakable feelings. I tucked those conflicting feelings away and walked around pretending that I didn't care one way or the other about his disease.

Since he declined the new treatment in Texas, my grandfather decided to move back to Roseville, which was in the Sacramento metropolitan area and about an hour away from Fairfield. He did so, with the desire to be close to family and friends while his health deteriorated. As expected his condition continued to worsen until he required oxygen to perform the most basic of daily functions.

I incorrectly assumed that once my grandfather was diagnosed, his illness would progress rapidly. But it didn't. He was often tired and would need to rest to preserve his strength. However, his health declined slowly. As a family, we had to deal with the fact that our patriarch was dying, but unlike the others, I also had to contend with feelings of remorse and guilt. I wanted it to all end; I wanted to bury him so those feelings could die with him.

Being as he was back in California, I had to often be in my grandfather's presence. During those times, I was always friendly and behaved as if our history wasn't our own. The life I lived taught me how to pretend very well. I was adept at convincing others that everything was okay. It had become second nature.

In my heart of hearts, I knew that I wasn't supposed to wish death upon anyone, but during my grandfather's sickness, I wondered why it was taking so long for him to pass. I was anxious to live a life without a cloud of shame hanging over me. I just wanted to be normal. His presence had stirred emotions I fought tooth and nail to bury, and they weren't going away.

On what would be my grandfather's last day alive, my mother and aunts gathered at his bedside. Somehow my mother knew that day would be his last. Earlier that morning, she called my father and told him to come say his goodbyes. Ever the family man, and still unaware that he had abused me, my father drove an hour to my grandfather's. For some reason, he did not take my brother and me with him. I believe my mother wanted her and her sisters to be the only ones to comfort their father on his last day. Presumably, she needed her husband for support. Whatever the reason, my father was there for her.

He would later tell me that he walked into my grandfather's room to find him accompanied by hospice care. He laid quietly in bed with his glassy eyes wide open. My father bent over his deathly ill father-in-law, and whispered in his ear, "Now I'm the only man left in the family to protect your daughters and your wife." It was a small and kind gesture meant to reassure my grandfather that he could rest easy knowing that his family would be taken care of. Not long after the brief shared moment, my father left, and my grandfather died an hour later.

My father always took pride in his final words to my grandfather, because he was able to give him peace of mind before he died. The first time, he expressed this to me my stomach turned. I felt nauseous. Because my mother had chosen to keep him in the dark, he unknowingly granted comfort to the man who repeatedly molested his daughter. The look of satisfaction in my father's eye ate me up inside.

My grandfather passed away September 08, 2008. At the reading of his last will and testament, there was no mention of either my brother or me. All of his worldly possessions had been left to my grandmother, mother, and aunts. It's funny because growing up, I remember thinking as long as I kept his secret he would have the decency to include me in his will. I never envisioned an amount because it wasn't about greed or bribery. Instead, I kept his secret because I didn't want to destroy my family. I was loyal to those who showed absolutely no loyalty to me. Still, I thought if he couldn't be loyal in life; he would do it in death. I was wrong, and yet again disappointed by my grandfather.

I didn't know how much my mother received, but she gave me five hundred dollars from her inheritance. I was well aware that she didn't have to give me anything, but knowing how well off my grandfather was, I'm sure she received thousands. And somehow, knowing what she knew, she deemed me worthy of five hundred dollars. It was a slap in the face. Needless to say, I took the small lump sum of money and set off to make a life for myself; one that held healing and a promising future.

My family did not have a funeral for my grandfather; he was cremated. Half of his ashes were scattered in the waters of Santa Cruz, where he could rest amongst the waves. What remained of his ashes was enshrined in a beautiful ball of crystal that resembled a star-filled galaxy. My mother, aunts, and grandmother each took turns displaying the ball in their homes. On the occasions it was in our home, I was grateful that my mother opted to keep it in her bedroom. I didn't want to look at it.

One morning, when she was in possession of my grandfather's ashes, my mother frantically called me to her room. She yelled, "Aleesha, Aleesha come in my room quick!" Her tone beckoned me, and I ran swiftly to her room. I arrived to find her lights abnormally flickering. Though there was a myriad of reasons why it could be happening, my mother was certain it had something to with my grandfather. She said, "I think its Opa visiting me!" She began to talk to the lights, hoping to receive an answer. "Dad is that you?" she asked. Astonishingly enough, the light flickered in a manner that could easily be interpreted as a response. That was all the confirmation she needed to know that her father was still with her in spirit. While she was elated with his visit, all I could think was, *Why can't he just leave me alone?!* Even in death, he could not let me be, and it angered me. When the lights returned to normal, I left my mother's room allowing her to relish in the fact that she regained contact with her deceased father whom I hated for ruining my childhood.

It had taken four years for my grandfather to succumb to his illness. Before he died, I finished high school. I graduated from Fairfield High in 2005 and was excited to start a new life. I aimed to free myself from any disappointment, guilt or shame. Most importantly, I strove to leave the scars of sexual abuse behind me. It was with great pride that I walked across my high school's stage and accepted my diploma. I had beaten the odds. I endured so much and overcame my troubled teen years to become a high school graduate.

Subsequent to graduation, I got a job at Safeway, a national supermarket chain, making sandwiches in the deli department. I hated that job, and I wanted more for myself. My problem was I didn't know exactly what I wanted; I simply knew there had to be better than what I was doing.

In 2006, at the age of nineteen, I moved out of my parent's house and into my own apartment. By this time I was a mail processing clerk at the United States Postal Service. From the time I was nineteen to twenty-one-years-old, I worked at the post office creating a life for myself. I no longer had to bend to whims of my grandfather or those who tried to protect him. My life was finally my own, and I was happy. That was until I had the unfortunate luck of meeting yet another man, who attempted to control me with fear and intimidation.

I was at work when an older Latino man approached me accusing me of stealing his jacket the previous day. He reasoned since I was the only one in the break room, I had to be the culprit. Of course, his accusation was completely unfounded. Eventually, he found his coat underneath the company's couch, yet remained adamant that I had something to do with it originally disappearing. As he continued to bombard me with accusations, I stood puzzled by his nonsensical reasoning. I was especially confused with his anger considering he had found his jacket. But still, I listened to his rant. In broken English, he explained that his time card was in his jacket pocket, and since he couldn't initially find it, he had to clock out of work late. As a result of his unauthorized late clock out, he received disciplinary actions from the higher-ups. All the while he was explaining himself; I was wondering what this had to do with me. I hoped he was just venting his frustrations and everything would eventually blow over since he had his jacket. Boy, did I misjudge the situation.

The following night, he furiously approached me and told me that if his jacket ever came up missing again, both my car and I would suffer the same fate. I was taken aback by his hostility toward me, particularly since I had nothing to do with the disappearance of his jacket. Something in me clicked. I decided that I would not be made to live in fear nor would allow anyone to subject me to any type of abuse. I had suffered in silence for far too long. I knew that I had to tell somebody.

I immediately informed my supervisor, in detail, about the entire ordeal. I noticed after my statement was taken and a few others were interviewed, the man was not at work the next day. I presumed he had been fired. About a month later, thirty days to be exact, I looked up from sorting mail to find my aggressor wearing an eerie smile and standing in front of me. His smile, which was the type that usually indicated malice or mischief, sent chills up my spine. It was a smile with which I was all too familiar. Without a second thought, I leaped from my seat and found a supervisor. That's when I was informed that as a result of a clerical error he was allowed to return to work. The post office mandated that he was to receive paperwork outlining the consequence of his actions within thirty days; he received it in thirty-one. I was speechless, but I refused to accept abusive behavior from another man. There was no way that I would continue to allow him to compromise my safety and mental welfare.

When I was a child, I had no choice but to deal with my grandfather's abusive behavior, but I was no longer a child. I was an adult and had control over what I would and would not accept in my life. Abuse was abuse, whether it was sexual, verbal or physical. I wasn't going to let my co-worker have an effect on the new life I was building for myself. I was more determined than ever to live free from mental anguish and stand tall while being fearless.

Due to the new stress, I decided to take a leave of absence from work. I filed the necessary paperwork with the post office to protect myself from the lunatic who had threatened to take my life. The documents were tedious, but it was well worth it. In the end, I was granted my request, and in 2007 I was authorized to take a leave of absence based on workplace stress. The timing of my leave could not have been better. To that point, I had dealt with all of my problems on my own, without any assistance from a professional, and it was beginning to take a serious toll on me.

On July 22, 2009, I received the blessing of all blessings; I became a mother. The first time I held Kalani in my arms, I accepted that from that moment she was my utmost responsibility. I didn't know it all, and there was no manual on motherhood that would ensure that I would always get everything right. But what I did know was from her first breath it became my full-time responsibility to make sure she never experienced the same pain as I had. When our eyes met, I saw myself in her features. My reflection told me that I wanted to raise her to be strong and aware of the cruelties that life could throw her way.

Her father was a high school love that didn't work. Our separation was no one's fault; we simply grew apart with time and age. After careful consideration, we decided to split when Kalani was around one-year-old. Although our relationship had ended, a beautiful baby girl came from our young love.

My love for Kalani was pure and magical; it fueled me like nothing before had ever done. She was and still is, my everything. I made an unbreakable vow to never let her down. As her mother, I took an oath to protect her at all cost; something my own mother failed to do. So I pushed harder to make a better life for the two us.

At the age of twenty-three, I decided that it was time to make a career change and enrolled at Solano College, a local school in Fairfield. I took early childhood education classes and became a preschool teacher at KinderCare, a national childcare chain. It was gratifying to be a part of an organization that had a great reputation. I worked for the company for one year before old feelings of being unfulfilled returned.

In 2013 I left KinderCare and moved to Los Angeles to help a friend pursue a career in rap. I acted in the capacity of her assistant. Together, we religiously promoted her music. We frequented studios and anywhere else that we thought would lead to her being discovered. I dedicated myself to her and her dream. I enjoyed every minute of helping her along the way.

As time went on my friend and I started bickering as friends who spend an exorbitant amount of time often do. In the beginning, our spats were never serious, but before long they progressed into physical altercations. Somehow, without me noticing, I had allowed abuse to once again enter my life. At that point, I knew our arrangement would no longer work. It simply wasn't conducive to my life, and I definitely didn't want my daughter living in that type of environment. So I left Los

Angeles and returned to the Bay Area to make a new and improved life plan.

Upon my return to the Bay Area, I reluctantly moved back in with my parents. They weren't getting along at the time and suffice it to say, our relationship was not at its best. I still harbored ill will that my mother knew about my abuse and brushed it under the rug. On the other hand, my father was strict at times, and his disciplinarian strained our relationship. Nevertheless, I didn't have anywhere else to go so I sucked it up and made sure that my return to Fairfield would be beneficial.

I reassessed my life and in the process noticed that I had developed a pattern of taking care of others before I took care of myself; Kalani excluded of course. I went from protecting my grandfather's feelings before my own, to taking care of my students at KinderCare. From there I helped a friend pursue a dream that most would deem unreachable. I had lost count how many times I had done this. I was neglecting myself and my needs. It was time for me to discover who I was. In order to do that, I had to stop putting my feelings aside and start living in my truth.

# CHAPTER NINE

*The road to healing from childhood sexual abuse is often an arduous path. Along the way, the abused are put in the position of reliving the horrific events of their pasts. However, with professional help, they can come to terms with their abuse and emerge survivors.*

In a perfect world, if a person is struggling to cope with pain, someone would always be there to help. But the world is not perfect, far from it, in fact. In many cases, those who have been hurt are left to put themselves back together from the pieces their perpetrator has left behind. That was me. I was alone in my healing process. Those around me, who knew of my abuse, had forsaken me long ago. I couldn't talk to my family. It was pointless to talk to my mother, and my father still had no idea what I had been through. So I took on the task of helping and bettering myself; by myself.

In 2014 I was living in my parent's home with my five-year-old daughter. I was lost but desperately sought to find my way. However, I had no idea what I wanted to with my life. I had job experience in various fields and numerous certifications. Still, I didn't know how or where I would apply my acquired skills.

One day while leisurely looking at Instagram posts, I happened upon a photo that piqued my interest. It was a woman wearing a body chain draped around her neck and waist. The accessory caught my immediate attention, and something came over me. Precisely at that moment, I decided that I would make body chains; then market and sell them on my social media pages. For a year straight, while still living with my parents, I made body chains. As a part of my promotional strategy, I attended events in the Bay Area and networked with celebrities. For once in my life, I was promoting myself instead of putting others before me, and it felt great.

From January 2014 to January 2015, every day of the 365 included, I sat in my parent's garage to escape the world around me and prayed. I did it irrespective if I was having a good or bad day. Growing up I didn't know much about God or His teachings. All I knew was what I was told; God was supposed to fix things if you read the Bible. At least that's how I was led to believe my grandfather would be cured. So when God never fixed him, I felt God had let me down. It wasn't until I became an adult and I got to know Him for myself that I came to have a better understanding of Him. It was then that I began to believe in God again.

I had my most profound conversations with God in my parent's garage. My prayers began with me asking, "God, what do you have me on Earth to do? Why am I here?" I knew living with my parents and making body jewelry was not why He put me on this Earth. My purpose had to be greater than what I was doing at the time.

The Bible says that patience is a virtue, and I am living proof of its truth. After 365 days of praying, God rewarded my patience by revealing to me what I needed to do with my life. It was right before my eyes the entire time, yet I had somehow overlooked it. I had a unique voice and perspective that could be used to help others like me; people who were victims of sexual abuse. I didn't have the faintest idea how everything would be implemented; however, my purpose was clear. I was going to seek to heal myself while helping others do the same. I was going to make strides to end child molestation and fight to ensure that those who preyed upon children were properly punished. And I was going to be a voice for the voiceless; one that reminded victims that their abuse was not their fault. My epiphany put my life in perspective; however, I could not start upon my new path until I told my father of my abuse.

## END SILENCED ABUSE: TELL SOMEBODY

In January 2015 after twenty-five years of marriage, my mother asked my father for a divorce. Her reason; she didn't love him anymore. News of the impending divorce sent a shockwave of pain through me; but not for the most obvious reason. Their divorce was a betrayal to me. For years, I suffered in silence under the premise that if I kept quiet my family would live happily ever after. Yet without regard to my sacrifice, my mother, the parent who knew of my abuse, decided she was done. Whereas I surrendered my childhood and chose others before myself out of naive obligation to family, she was ready to walk away and leave our destroyed family in her wake. For as much pain as it caused me, my mother's decision to divorce my father, released me from the responsibility of keeping my family together.

By the time my mother announced her plans for divorce, I was twenty-eight-years-old and only a select few, outside of my mother and aunts, knew of my abuse. When I was in my father's presence, the words often sat on the tip of tongue attempting to claw their way out, while I frantically bit them back. I wanted more than anything to blurt the truth out to get it over with, but I was too nervous. I built the necessary courage by confiding in my cousin that I was ready to tell my father, but was confused on how to do it. After she shared a few encouraging words, we ended our conversation with me feeling hopeful.

Three days later my father and I were in the family kitchen when he casually started a conversation with me. We talked of nothing of too much importance before I noticed a shift in his tone of voice. I prepared myself. If his tone were any indication, our conversation would take a serious turn. However, there was nothing that could have ever prepared me for my father's words. He solemnly faced me and explained that my younger brother Jayson had confided that our grandfather had molested him his entire childhood. My father continued to say that the guilt had become too much for Jayson to bear and since my mother had broken the family up, he could now tell of his abuse without the worry of destroying the family in the process.

The world stopped around me and disappeared except for my father's voice. As he spoke, I willed myself to turn away from him so he would not bear witness to the emotions that overcame me. I couldn't believe it; how could I have not known. Not once did it occur to me that my grandfather would ever touch my brother. I never thought about what he was doing when he wasn't molesting me; I was just thankful for the time free of him. All of those years I thought it was just me, and it infuriated me that he had gotten his hands on my little brother. If my mother and aunts would have done more when I told them about my abuse, then my Jayson would have never fallen prey to my grandfather. Tears streamed down my face. I cried for myself, and I cried for my brother. And then a voice as clear as if He was standing beside me, God said to me, "This is your time to tell." With a face full of tears I turned back to face my father. Without me saying a word, he knew; he saw the answer to his question before he asked it, yet he asked it all the same.

"Did your grandfather touch you?" I lowered my head. The tears that had seconds ago flowed like a steady stream burst from me as I cried uncontrollably. Through gasps, I told my father everything; including how my mother knew. My father jumped from the barstool where he sat and hugged me tightly. Together we stood in the kitchen and cried. His heart broke for both my brother and me. But he was also furious.

His anger for my mother was palpable. He wondered out loud how she and her family could know such a thing was happening and do nothing to stop it. It was hard for him to comprehend how his wife could lay next to him every night and keep such a vile secret. Like him, I didn't have an answer. That night, with my truth finally free, my father and I allowed the sadness to envelop us.

Days later, his sadness gave way to anger. "Why didn't you tell me when you were a child?" he yelled. "I could have saved you!" Before I could answer, he continued. "You should have said something because when it happened to me, I didn't have a choice."

His words hung in the air as I stood with my mouth agape waiting for him to explain.

When he began to speak again, he was no longer yelling. "When I was a child growing up in Louisiana I was molested by my preacher at the church."

My eyes widened as I attentively listened to each word he spoke.

"He used to take me into a secluded room where he would give me the communion wine to get me intoxicated," he said. "Once I was, he took advantage of me by touching me, and when he was finished, he would tell me not to say a word to anyone. I did exactly that, and never told anyone. Back then you didn't tell on a preacher, especially if he was white. Nothing probably would have happened if I did considering the lack of rights black people had back then. So you see I didn't have a choice, but you did, you could have come to me, I would have saved you."

When my father finished speaking, a stillness fell over the room and time stopped as we were each locked in the other's gaze. My entire childhood, I had been led to believe that he would never understand if I told him of my abuse, and years later I found out that he would have understood more than anyone else. His body language spoke of defeat. In his stance I could see he believed he failed me by not protecting me. I added it to the list of things my grandfather ruined. The silence between us was finally broken when I mumbled, "It wasn't that easy to come and tell you, especially as a child."

Over the next few days, my father's mood understandably varied as he processed the news my brother and I shared with him. It goes without saying that I understood. It was a lot to handle, especially since the timing of the revelations coincided with his impending divorce.

By this time my mother and father were living in separate homes, therefore, when he called her to come over she naturally assumed it was to finalize details of the divorce. Upon her arrival, my mother looked relaxed as she sat with her fingers interlaced and legs crossed waiting to hear what my father had to say. My father played it cool for as long he could but was ultimately unable to hide disdain for her actions. He let her know that my brother and I had come forward with abuse allegations against her father, and he knew the part she and her sisters played in the cover-up.

Any semblance of composure she had vanished. My mother's spine stiffened, and the color drained from her face. She was quiet for a moment, before admitting that I had indeed come to her about my abuse. My mother went on to say that she and her sisters confronted their father and threatened to contact the police if he continued to sexually assault me. By her account, she thought my grandfather had stopped molesting me because I never mentioned anything about it again.

The more she spoke, the more her admission gradually transformed into a defense of her actions. She told my father that upon finding out I was abused by my grandfather, she immediately took me to counseling, but stopped once I told her I didn't want to go. I thought she surely had to be mistaken. I could vividly remember being sexually abused from the age of six to fourteen, but for the life of me, I couldn't remember ever going to a counseling session. It wasn't fathomable to believe that my mother, the same woman who encouraged me to keep my abuse a secret, would take me to a complete stranger to discuss its effects upon me. I simply could not find any truth in her story, and as I contemplated this thought my father's screams pulled me back into their conversation. In the end, he was disgusted beyond words. The only ones he could muster were for her to take every one of her belongings from the home they once shared and never to return.

My mother grabbed what she could and left the house in a hurry. I stood by silently as I watched the scene I had long tried to avoid, play out in front of my eyes. The mood of the room was heavy, and I was an emotional wreck. But something had changed in me. After my conversation with my father, I was able to break free from the shame and guilt I had carried for years. However, as I watched my mother walk out the door, I shed the pains of my childhood. The little girl that was once lost and scared found herself, and she was destined to make her mark in the world.

Just as my mother was getting into her car to drive away, my father told me that I needed to go outside and get the answers that I was owed. I wholeheartedly agreed. I rushed outside and caught her right in the nick of time. As she was about to drive off, I yelled at the top of my lungs, "Why did you let it happen to me?"

She stopped the car, rolled down her window and screamed, "I never knew that it was continuing. I'm sorry, what do you want from me?"

I didn't know what to say; I didn't have an answer for her question. So I stood there with a blank face and closed mouth as she drove off. When I was nothing more than a figure in her rearview mirror I went back inside to find my father still visibly upset. With my mother's confirmation of all involved in my grandfather's cover-up, he encouraged me to call my grandmother and two aunts.

I called my grandmother first, but she didn't answer. However, I would not allow that to stop me from saying what I needed to say. I left her a message saying, "Oma, it's hard for me to believe that you didn't know what was going on. You were a stay at home wife and mother. How did this slip under your nose; going unnoticed for years? You never had a job. How did you not see the signs that your husband was molesting my brother and me?" I finished my message and hung up the phone.

Although my messaged conveyed what I was thinking, I simply could not let her get off that easy. I needed to speak to her, not her voicemail. Accordingly, I called repeatedly until she answered. Being as I was speaking to my grandmother, I tried my best not be disrespectful, but I was livid. In the nicest tone possible I explained what her husband had done to me; to which she claimed to have no knowledge. According to her, she never witnessed any clues or signs that pointed to him being a child molester. Regret tinged her voice when she expressed disappointment in my grandfather for never confiding in her, not even on his deathbed because, in her words, she would have wanted to hear the truth from him.

Out of respect, I listened to my grandmother; however, I knew, without any doubt she was always 'Team Theodorus Bernardus Dejong.' The more she spoke, the easier it became to see that she was preparing his defense. As anticipated, she attempted to shift blame away from him by telling me he, too, had been molested as a child. She said when my grandfather was a little boy, a strange man exposed himself to him on a daily basis while he played soccer in the park. Admittedly, it helped me to understand why he did what he did; it was a learned behavior. Though it brought clarity, it did not absolve him of wrongdoing. I let my grandmother finish all she had to say; still in disbelief that she didn't know about my molestation. But doubting her would get me nowhere as I had no way of disproving anything she said. I needed to call someone who could give me straight answers. I decided to call my aunt who lived in Texas; the first person I told. I would later discover that she was also the first person my brother told. She let both of us down.

When she answered the phone, I couldn't feign the pleasantries one typically exchanges on a call. I got straight to the matter at hand. "How could you feed my little brother and me to the wolf?" I asked without waiting for an answer before continuing. "How dare you sit back and do nothing to help when I told you I was being sexually abused. Not only did I come to you but my younger brother confided in you as well just a couple of years after I did, and you did absolutely nothing." It infuriated me to know that my favorite aunt, who at one point could do no wrong in my eyes, failed both my brother and me. Unlike with my grandmother and mother, I cursed and yelled. I couldn't contain my anger. It was the first time that I could direct my rage towards those who wronged me, and I wasn't holding back.

In the midst of the mutual screaming and yelling, I heard her say that I never told her that I was sexually abused as a child. That was a blatant lie! In keeping with her fabricated version of events, she said that I told my mother first, and my mother told her. Her words cut like a knife. I hadn't been the victim of such traitorous behavior since the adults in my life ignored my pleas for help as I was being abused. How dare she imply that I was lying and even worse attempt to make herself look like she was powerless to help me. I was the victim, not her!

With each lie told she treated me as if I were still a fragile, naive six-year-old who would believe anything I was told. She told lie after lie until I couldn't take it anymore. I cut her off; I had to. She was a liar, and I told her as such. I expected her to yell at me in return, but I in no way expected her response. She told me that she was molested as a child too and since it happened to her, then I needed to get over it as she eventually did. My mouth dropped to learn that for the fourth time that another family member had been sexually abused. After her confession, my aunt stopped yelling and spoke in a more conversational tone. She advised that I seek both professional help and spiritual guidance from Jesus; then hung up.

I didn't know how to take her admission. However, for the most part, it stung terribly. How was it possible for her to be a victim of child molestation and not empathize with me at all? Try as I might, I couldn't wrap my mind around it. It exhausted me to even try; the conversation alone had taken all of my energy. My father would have to wait to find out what happened. I had nothing left; I needed a second to myself.

When I finally gathered the energy to give my father the details of my conversation with my aunt he was incredulous. He asked, "Where were her Christian guidance and counseling when you went to her at the age of six for help?" I agreed, and his fire gave me the drive to make my next phone call.

I approached the call with my mother's youngest sister in the same manner I had with my other aunt. "How could you let Jayson and me get sexually abused by your father and not help us?" I asked as soon as she answered. Like her sister before her, she yelled that she didn't let it happen before hanging up. Where one would think that being hung up on for the second time, by the second aunt would infuriate me, it actually saddened me. At that point, it became increasingly clear that I had no value in my family. Why were they so angry at me, when I was the one who was hurt? Their father had molested me; I hadn't done a thing to them.

A minute later my aunt called me back. The hard edge was gone from her voice; instead, her tone was kind and warm. She spoke of finding out that I was being molested and opening her home to me for a few days. While I was there, she held and comforted me. She did her best to ensure that I felt loved and secure. I listened attentively as my aunt revealed that the next time she saw her father, she let him know that if she ever heard he was touching me again, she would call the cops and have him arrested. Then she did the unexpected; she apologized. Although she did what she thought was right at the time, she realized that she could have done more.

Before we ended our call, she expressed her love for me and the desire to continue our relationship despite the ugliness that surrounded it at the time. I sincerely appreciated her for the kind words, because they were more than anyone else had given me. The earlier tension between us had subsided. Her words rang with earnest intent, and the apology felt genuine; therefore I accepted it. I got off the call pleased that it ended on a good note, and held the hope that eventually I could speak to the rest of my family as I had my aunt. However, I didn't get my hopes up.

# CHAPTER NINE

The tension between my mother and father continued to fester as their divorce proceedings moved forward. Their once harmonious existence turned contentious, particularly on the part of my father as he harbored ill-feelings toward my mother for her involvement in protecting my grandfather. Though I played no part in my mother's decision to file for divorce, I couldn't ignore that my revelation had added fuel to the fire. Still, I refused blame for myself for the actions of others. Even though I would have preferred for my parents to stay together, it was their choice, and for once in my life, I chose to focus on me and my goal to bring awareness to child molestation.

As the first step in my plan of action, I posted a video on my Facebook and Instagram pages introducing myself and confessing that I was molested by my grandfather.

With the assistance of my daughter Kalani, who was five at the time, I followed up by posting a guide instructing parents how to teach their children about their untouchable body parts. In the video, Kalani and I discussed her body including her four private areas; her mouth, chest, vagina, and behind. I further explained that no one should ever touch any of her private areas, and if someone did, she was to tell me. The feedback was overwhelmingly positive. Parents wrote to tell me that with the help of my video they were able to sit with their children and discuss the difficult subject matter. On the whole, they were grateful for the video, and I was, in turn, not only happy but proud to give it to them.

After posting my first two videos, I received a message that I wished I never had to receive; but all things considered, I was pleased to have been able to make a difference. A mother messaged me on Facebook and told me that her three-year-old daughter, after watching my video, revealed that her uncle was molesting her. Tears streamed down my face as I read the stranger's message. As opposed to past experiences, my tears were of both joy and pain. I was abundantly happy to know the little girl found enough comfort in my words to tell her mother she was being abused. But at the same time, it upset me to know that she had to suffer such an ordeal. Then my videos became a beacon of sorts for the abused, and I began to receive numerous messages, some of which were surprisingly from people I did know.

## END SILENCED ABUSE: TELL SOMEBODY

I was shocked to find a message from my high school friend, the same friend whose house I would often visit and with who I defaced the principal's plaque. He reached out to me and shared that his male babysitter, in addition to his mother and father, had sexually abused him throughout his childhood. I always had a feeling that the two of us shared a bond beyond similar ethnic makeup, but I never would have imagined that our commonality lied in abuse. Who knows how we could have helped each other if we had only trusted our friendship enough to speak about what was going on in our homes. We probably could have saved each other a lot of pain, but there was no need to dwell on the past. Instead, I focused on the fact that he had the courage to speak out when he did.

Yet another high school friend sent me a message and shared that she had been molested by her uncle. She wanted to tell her parents. However they were both in extremely poor health, and she didn't want to bring them any undue stress. In light of her unique circumstances and taking her parents' health into account, I agreed that she should consider refraining from telling them.

Later that night, I discussed my day with my father, including how I was contacted by two high school friends and the advice I had given one of them. He listened carefully, before telling me that I was wrong for dispensing such bad advice. His words stunned me; nevertheless, I listened as he fully explained that even on his deathbed he would want to know what happened to his children. I understood where he was coming from but still found myself sympathetic to the plight of her parents. My father must have sensed my hesitation to agree with his point of view. He then asked, "If anything ever happened to Kalani, wouldn't you want to know?" That one question put everything into perspective for me, and I conceded the point.

He suggested that I write to my friend and advise her to *tell* because it was the right thing to do. I replayed my father's advice in my head. Each time his emphasis on the word *tell* was unmistakable. It sparked something inside of me. It served as a reminder that when I was being molested by my grandfather, all I wanted to do was to *tell* someone; anyone who would genuinely listen and release me from the hell in which I was living. I didn't know it at the time, but my father's sage advice, in all of its earnest simplicity, would become the blueprint for my nonprofit organization, *Tell Somebody, Inc.*

After years of harboring my secret, it was freeing to be able to speak openly with my father. I told him about the two videos I posted and the positive response they both received; including the one that elicited the advice we previously discussed. My father beamed with pride. He commended Kalani and me for doing our part to educate the parents and children on such an important topic. He was, however, outraged that no one had yet to take accountability for the abuse I suffered. He then suggested that I use the subject for the topic of my next video and offered an idea how I could go about it. I began to think of all the reasons why a video on accountability might not have been the best thing to do until he spoke of my daughter. He reminded me of all that I would do to protect her and how someone should have done the same for me.

With those words, it all became clear. I was an adult, and I was doing the same thing I did as a child. I was putting my family's feelings before mine, and I was tired of it. With the exception of my mother's youngest sister, no one in the family even had the decency to have a civilized conversation regarding how they failed me.

On January 31, 2015, I posted the video that officially introduced *Tell Somebody, Inc.* to the world. In a matter of a few weeks, I began the journey to reclaim my life with no plan to slow down.

Approximately a month later, on February 16, 2015, I posted a ten-minute video that delved into the part my family played in protecting and enabling my pedophilic grandfather; thereby facilitating years of my abuse. Even though my grandfather was the only person to ever molest me; his wife and his daughters were complicit. And for that, they were as guilty as he was. Initially, the thought of bringing their transgressions to light, gave me great pause until I remembered that I had nothing to lose. At that point, my mother and her family had all but disowned me. Not only had they changed their phone numbers, but I was also blocked on their social media pages. I was persona non-grata. Besides at the root, the video wasn't about them. It never was. It was about other victims of sexual abuse; the response to my first videos had proven that. I just prayed that it wasn't all in vain.

I prefaced my message by holding up a family picture of my grandfather, grandmother, aunts, mother and me as a baby. I pointed to each of our faces and shared our names one by one. Then I told my story and the role each person in picture played in my abuse. I used my story to convey the importance of not allowing child molesters to hide in the shadows and comfort created by anonymity and collusion. Someone needed to shed light on them, and I was that person; however, I needed the help of my viewers. I sent out an impassioned plea for anyone who had suffered or was currently suffering from child molestation or any other type of sexual abuse to tell somebody because it was time for all of us to heal.

After I posted the video, I sat with my eyes glued to the computer screen, refreshing it every other second waiting for the first comment. Suddenly, I received hundreds of friend requests, and the number of views for my post increased tenfold. In just a short time my video accumulated over a hundred thousand views and fifty thousand shares. While I expected it to get some attention, I was pleasantly surprised that viewers were watching not a one-minute video, but a ten-minute video in its entirety.

As the messages poured in, I read some of them aloud. They were from hundreds of people, each sharing stories similar to mine. Many of them who sent messages thought they were alone, and in viewing my video, they found comfort in discovering they weren't. I was overwhelmed by the words of my kindred spirits. All the nervousness, shame, guilt, and disgust that invariably laid just below the surface and colored all of my everyday interactions, began to dissipate. As boastful as it may sound, I felt like a hero; and *Tell Somebody Inc.* was just getting started.

I purchased customized t-shirts with the words "Tell Somebody" across the front for Kalani, my father and me. I was inexpressibly excited by the prospect of distributing similar shirts to family members who were supportive of my cause. I enthusiastically posted a picture of the three of us in our crisp *Tell Somebody* t-shirts. I never imagined that the response to the photo would not only be immediate, but remarkably positive. It received over 100 thousand likes, 25 thousand shares and fifty thousand comments from different people. Not only were viewers continuing to share their stories, but they were also inquiring where they could purchase the *Tell Somebody* t-shirt.

It began to occur to me that if my posts could elicit such considerable responses, I could reach many more with a bigger platform; television. I faithfully wrote letters to *Dr. Phil*, *Steve Harvey*, and *Ellen* every day. *The*

*Oprah Winfrey Show* no longer aired, but I nonetheless wrote to its former host, just like I did the others, hoping she would relate to *Tell Somebody* since she too was a victim of sexual abuse as a child.

On February 26, 2015, I received a letter from *Dr. Phil* expressing the show's interest in having me as a guest; to which I wholeheartedly agreed. I was ecstatic that my persistence has paid off and excitedly anticipated appearing on the show. Prior to taping the show's producers called me to discuss their expectations for my appearance. The euphoria of receiving my invite waned when the producer informed me that either my mother, grandmother or one of my aunts had to appear alongside me to foster a complete discussion on my abuse. I knew their request would be difficult to honor by virtue of the fact that my mother's side of the family wasn't speaking to me. Still, I didn't become discouraged. I remained hopeful and left the matter in God's hands.

Despite the minor setback, I called my father and shared my good news, including the unexpected turn of events. My father, who was as realistic as he was proud of me, cautioned me not to get my hopes up that anyone in my mother's family would appear on the show. I strongly disagreed with him. I truly believed that once they understood I was trying to help others by bringing awareness to the importance of speaking up about sexual abuse, they would consider joining me on *Dr. Phil*. My father remained unconvinced, which made me want to more than ever prove him wrong.

I opted to call my mother first. Instead of hearing the tepid *hello* I expected, I heard, "We're sorry you have reached a number that has been disconnected or is no longer in service. If you feel you have reached this recording in error, please check the number and try your call again." I took my cellphone phone away from my ear and checked the number as the automated message suggested. I had dialed the correct number. Working under the assumption that it was just one of those things that sometimes happened, I called once more. Again, the automated message played. Undeterred I sent texts to my aunts and grandmother because I figured it gave my message the best chance of being received. My messages relayed the same information I would have, had they answered their phones. They said we had the opportunity to save millions by sharing our story on *Dr. Phil*.

I eagerly awaited by my phone, keeping my fingers crossed that at least one of them would agree to be on *Dr. Phil* with me. My mother's youngest sister was the first to respond. Taking into account that she was apologetic when I last confronted her, I assumed she would be more than willing to help me out. I was wrong. She didn't say no, nor did she say yes. She said that she would have to think about it.

After it was clear that neither my grandmother nor other aunt was going to respond to my text, I became desperate. My mother was my last hope of appearing on *Dr. Phil*. I took it upon myself to drive forty-five minutes to my mother's place of employment. Unfortunately, I made the drive in vain, being as she wasn't at work that day. While driving home, I called her dedicated line at work and left a message. It worked; she called me the next day and congratulated me on the great things that were happening in my life. But in the end, she didn't want to attend the taping with me. My mother rationalized that since I was abused such a long time prior, she wouldn't be able to remember all of the details, and for the many of the things she did remember, she didn't have an answer. Besides, she didn't want to be painted as a terrible mother on national television because she couldn't remember. While I appreciated my mother returning my call, I was disappointed in not only her decision to not to help me but also the realization that my father and Kalani were truly the only two family members in my corner.

When I received the call from *Dr. Phil*, I foresaw national recognition for *Tell Somebody,* but it just wasn't my time. I would be lying if I said the missed opportunity wasn't a huge blow, but I wasn't going to let the misstep deter me from my mission. I had faith that God had big plans for me and vowed to be ready when my time came. Therefore I shifted my focus to what I could do on a grassroots level.

I couldn't reach Dr. Phil's viewers, but I could reach the survivors of sexual abuse in my area who had contacted me via social media. I figured it would be therapeutic if we, as survivors, came together and supported one another's healing. That is how the *Tell Somebody Barbecue* came to be. I marked March 14, 2015, on my calendar as the big day.

To my surprise, a day before the barbecue I was contacted by KRON 4 News, from the local Bay Area television station. They wanted to do a special on my life and the *Tell Somebody* movement, and they would be at my home in an hour! Adrenaline pumped through my veins as I ran to tell my father the great news.

Due to the rushed circumstances, I didn't have much time to tidy up my home and get dressed. However, I was in rare form and successfully pulled it all together before KRON 4 News arrived. My hair wasn't at its best nor was my makeup precise, but I didn't care. I wasn't trying to make a fashion statement; I was trying to change the world. My father, daughter and I beamed with pride and looked at one another with absolute admiration as the three of us slipped into our *Tell Somebody* t-shirts and waited patiently for the news crew to arrive.

After what seemed like a few passing moments, a female reporter pulled up to my home in a red compact car. I watched through the blinds as she walked up to my door holding a camera. Once introductions and other the formalities were out of the way, the reporter suggested that she conduct the interview in the same park where I would host the *Tell Somebody Barbecue*. Just before the interview started, the reporter expressed the importance of not directly or indirectly naming my abuser. Naturally, I complied with her request because it was more important to get my message out than to mention names. Although extremely excited, I was nervous during the interview, but I refused to let my nerves get the best of me. I spoke of my story and cause with the utmost confidence. I was on an emotional high.

When the interview wrapped and we returned home, my excitement had not subsided in the least. So I asked my father if I could interview him on the topic and he happily obliged. I pressed the record button on my phone and asked if there was anything he wanted to say. The first things out of his mouth were the exact words he spoke the night I confided in him about my abuse and mother. He said, "I can't believe my wife of twenty-five years laid next to me every night and told me she loved me was keeping this deep dark secret from me the whole time." And I thought he was finished, but he continued, "Aleesha keep doing what you're doing. Keep advocating because somebody has to do it. I'm so proud of you." The sincerity of his words touched me. Additionally, he did such a great job with his interview that I thought it was a good idea to reshoot a video I made of him the previous week; especially since he was wearing his *Tell Somebody* t-shirt. Somehow my father sensed I wouldn't want to post a video with the dirty dishes; so he promised that he would redo the video for me at a later date. Although I had a feeling that we should have done the video immediately, I agreed with reluctance to wait as my father suggested.

# CHAPTER TEN

I woke up the morning of March 14, 2015, with the sense that there would be a great turnout for my *Tell Somebody Barbecue*; particularly since I had been featured on the news just the day before. I was certain there would be everyone from friends and family to survivors and supporters. I even expected there to be people who just happened upon the event and wanted to see what it was all about. In anticipation of the crowd, I purchased about 500 chicken drumsticks, 500 hot dogs; amongst other things. I spent a great deal of money on food for the event, but I didn't mind because it was important to me that everyone who attended the event had enough to eat. My brother Charles, who wanted to support me and my cause, manned the grill. He loved the idea of *Tell Somebody* and understood why I was adamant about advocating for victims of abuse. It was a cause close to his heart given that he was molested as a child by his caretaker's fifteen-year-old granddaughters. I was astounded when I found out but honored that he shared his truth with me. I was moved that he was angry that he was unable to protect me from my grandfather. Where so many had let me down, it was comforting to know that had he known, Charles would have protected me. But the reality is, he didn't live with us, and there wasn't much that he could do. Besides, he more than made up for his absence with everything he was doing for me, and I loved every minute of it.

Undeterred by the heat from the blazing sun, Charles, Kalani, my father and I, prepared for a large crowd and a successful event. By the time the *Tell Somebody Barbecue* began only a handful of people had shown up. At its conclusion, there were still only a handful of people, and most of them had accompanied me to the park. Although there were far fewer attendees than I expected, I extended my sincerest gratitude for the support of those who had shown up.

Seeing as we had prepared for hundreds, we had an abundance of food left. Collectively, we decided to donate the surplus of food to the local Fairfield homeless shelter. Seeing how grateful the residents of the shelter were to receive the hot dogs, Capri Suns, chips and chicken melted my heart. God always has a divine plan, and I was glad to be a part of one that day. Even though the barbecue didn't turn out as I had imagined, I was still able to help people that day, and it was a beautiful feeling.

Later that night, I had time to reflect on the events of the day, and it occurred to me why the *Tell Somebody Barbecue* hadn't attracted a large crowd. I realized that even though I was ready to tell my story, that doesn't mean others were automatically ready to tell theirs. My healing was my own, and other's had to heal in their own time. It was naïve of me to believe that because people supported me on social media, they would also want to meet me or reveal themselves publicly as victims of abuse. I slowly came to appreciate that for many, social media was a safe place to express pain because it allowed them to vent while maintaining anonymity. Truthfully, I was proud of my barbeque and accepted that the outcome was meant to be what it was. To better the situation, *Tell Somebody* was continuously building positive momentum.

On March 19, 2015, I was honored with an invitation to be a guest on Blog Talk Radio's *NMEMindz* hosted by ZaZa Ali and Professor Griff, who were both prolific figures in the community. I was delighted that they took an interest in the *Tell Somebody* movement, and gladly accepted their invitation. The *NMEMindz* interview was my first public radio interview, and despite my nerves, the conversation flowed naturally. For every question they asked, I effortlessly responded. I suppose it was because I was speaking my truth and knew the exact message I wanted to convey to listeners.

From that day forward, I met every interview request that I received; whether it was in person, over the telephone, or via Skype. Before I noticed it, *Tell Somebody* and I gained a lot of traction. And after years of having to be silent about my abuse, not a day passed that I didn't openly and freely talk about it. It was strange really because when I was a child, I tried every day to forget what my grandfather was doing to me and yearned to live a typical life. However, as an adult, I accepted that if I wanted to help others, I couldn't be allowed the luxury of forgetting. My story helped others heal and helping others helped to heal me.

I often spoke with my father and worked through my memories, so as not to forget any detail that would shape the advice I offered. The conversations with him were the best, and I loved talking to him because he didn't hold back. He told it like it was and kept me grounded. Therefore he unsurprisingly had great advice for me when I shared the story of how I purchased my first car. Being as I was young when it happened, I never truly gave much thought to the fact that others might not consider blackmailing my grandfather and mother the best way to get a car. And besides, it in no way negated the fact that he molested me. My father advised me to make a video, to tell the entire truth about the car before anyone else had a chance to. He reasoned that it would give the opportunity to explain why I did what I did, and he was right. It was the best thing to do. I didn't want to run the risk of discrediting *Tell Somebody* or my story. If taken the wrong way and without background, someone could discount the severity of my abuse because I received gifts from my grandfather.

As per his recommendation, I made a video detailing how I blackmailed my mother and grandfather when I was a teenager. I was sure to include my reasoning at the time and how, although I went through with it, I never thought it was okay. Before posting the video to my social media accounts, I wrapped it with a heartfelt and sincerest message to viewers discouraging anyone from resorting to blackmail. I asked them to instead learn from my mistake.

My father and I had a conversation crucial to the success of *Tell Somebody* on March 22, 2015. In the midst of him imparting wisdom, he said something to me that I should have seen before. He asked how was it that I was advocating for others to "tell somebody," when in fact I had not given a full statement to the police. His words were like a dagger through the heart, primarily because he was right. If I were going to lead, I would have it do it by example. So I got in my car and drove two hours to Foster City.

Over the course of the ride, I pondered upon the gravity of what I was about to do. It was scary and nerve-wracking, but it had to be done if I were going to be true to *Tell Somebody*. In a show of solidarity with my followers, I filmed my journey to the police station to file a report of my abuse. I did it because I didn't want them to solely hear me say tell somebody. I wanted them to see me tell somebody, or at the very least see my trip to do so. They needed to know that I wasn't asking them to do anything that I wasn't willing to do myself. I was pleased to demonstrate that it is never too late to tell.

Cameras weren't allowed in the police station; therefore, I had to stop filming before entering the building. With my head held high and a *Tell Somebody* t-shirt on my back, I walked into the police station and inquired about making a police report. The officer sat quietly and listened as details of my abuse spilled from my lips. She wrote down everything I said and asked for clarity on matters she didn't quite understand. And I genuinely appreciated that she seemed to be interested in not only helping me but listening, really listening, to me as well. The officer even asked about my shirt, and we had an in-depth conversation about *Tell Somebody* and its purpose. She admired my movement, complimented my bravery, and encouraged me to keep doing what I was doing before she stepped away. Her candor and reassuring words brought tears to my eyes. Then again I had cried the entire time I was there, from beginning to end.

When the officer returned, she informed me that in the State of California the statute of limitations was seven years for the crime perpetrated upon me. And since the time between the crime and my report exceeded seven years she would have to pass my file to the District Attorney's office, and they would determine if it was possible to proceed with the case. Defeated, I gathered my things and prepared to leave. Just before I exited the police station, the officer approached me holding a piece of paper. It wasn't just any piece of paper; it was the police report from 2003 when I was taken to the Fairfield Police Department for vandalism. In it was my statement that my grandfather had repeatedly molested me.

For years, I thought the report was a waste and did nothing to help. But there it was, reappearing years later. According to the officer, the Fairfield Police Department instructed my mother to continue my report at the Foster City Department, because it had jurisdiction. However, there was no record that she ever followed through. In fact, there was documentation that she and I never visited Foster City Police Department.

I left the police station feeling like a weight had been lifted off of my shoulders. The last little bits of shame, embarrassment, and guilt were left behind on that police report. Where I once felt defeated; I felt vindicated. Although the statute of limitations had lapsed, I accomplished what I set out to do. I reported my grandfather's crime and someone heard my story. While I drove, I continued recording where I had previously left off and encouraged others to do as I had just done; file a report. I implored them to take that step because even if the statute of limitations had passed the crime against them would be forever documented.

The sense of achievement that I felt was only exceeded by how proud my father was of me. He often told me how much he admired how I grew stronger with each passing day. His words of optimism and reassurance made it possible for me to look at myself in the mirror and actually believe that I had a chance to be me, instead of being known for what was done to me. With his help, I took back my life. It was the daily love and encouragement he gave me from the day I revealed my secret that kept me running full speed ahead. His love gave me the fortitude to grab others along the way, so we could all reach our goal to heal. He was my rock, my foundation, and my anchor. I didn't know where I would have been and what I would ever do without him. Sadly, on March 29, 2015, I had no choice but to figure it out.

That morning, for some reason, I was awakened at 6 a.m. and was unable to fall back asleep. My father was at work at the United States Postal Service, where he had been employed since he was honorably discharged from the Air Force. I restlessly tossed and turned for about two hours, until I finally found peace and fell asleep at 8:15 a.m. Around 11:15 a.m., after having slept for about only three hours, something woke me from my deep sleep. Still half-asleep I groggily, and what had to be at the hand of God, walked over to my bedroom window just in time to see a police car pull up and park in front of my house. My eyes stayed fixed as a man, who I would find out was a detective, got out of the unmarked car and walked toward my front door. Still in my pajamas, I dashed from my room in time to open the door before he could ring my doorbell. The detective's face immediately told me something was wrong. His attempt to hide his expression failed, but in those few minutes, I held on to the hope that I was mistaken. After what felt like hours, he finally spoke. "Hello is Charles Barlow here?" he asked sternly as he flashed his badge.

"Uh no, I believe he's at work," I replied.

"Can you do me a favor and go check for me?" he politely asked.

Although I found it rather odd that the detective wanted to know my father's whereabouts, I nonetheless did as he requested. I replied, "Yes hold on, give me one second while I go check," before I futilely walked away from the door. I knew my father wasn't home. It was Sunday morning, and he always worked Sundays for overtime. But I still checked. I went to his room knocked on his door; no answer. Satisfied that he wasn't there, I returned to inform the detective that my father must have still been at work and inquired if there was anything I could help him with.

He stood stoically before asking, "Is Mrs. Barlow home?"

I was taken aback by his question considering my mother and father had not lived together for quite some time. I informed the detective of this fact, and he responded by asking if he could come in. I motioned for him to enter and led him to the living room so we could discuss the nature of his visit. He sat, while I opted to stand. Once the detective was comfortable, he cleared his throat for the hundredth time and said, "I'm sorry to tell you this, but your father was in a car accident this morning, and he didn't make it."

I looked squarely at him and burst into laughter. "You're lying, right?" I asked.

He responded calmly, "I'm sorry I wish I were. This is the hardest part of my job. Your father was on his way home from work and crashed at approximately 8:15 a.m. this morning. The accident occurred just about five minutes up the road from your home. He lost control of his car, ran off the side of the road, and hit a tree. He died instantly."

As I listened to the detective, I couldn't help but notice that he said my father died at 8:15 a.m., the precise time I found the peace and sense of calm I needed to fall asleep. I quickly erased the thought from my head.

I asked again if he was lying and let out a light laugh. When the detective didn't respond, I laughed again and asked if he and my father were playing some type of prank. I looked down the hallway hoping my father would jump from behind the door and say, *got you!* As stern as my father could be, he had a wonderful sense of humor and could make even the meanest person crack a smile. And then reality struck.

I looked at the detective, who was sitting with his head lowered. In one hand he held my father's wallet and in the other hand were his car keys. I covered my mouth in an attempt to stifle my audible gasp. I couldn't let it escape me because I needed to continue to believe that what the detective said was untrue. I tried; I really tried. But then my eyes were drawn to my father's keys in the detective's hand. I noticed the ignition key was badly bent, and my world shattered.

I cried as the detective returned my father's belongings to me. He then gave me a card and suggested I call the coroner with any questions. He further explained that the California Highway Patrol had towed my father's car to rule out foul play and I would have to wait thirty days to receive a report outlining the full details about his death. Thirty days?!

The detective placed his hand on my shoulder and in a gesture of kindness gave it what was to be a comforting squeeze. I'm almost certain he offered his condolences, but I couldn't hear above my internal screams of agony. I went through the motions, without much thought, and made the appropriate gestures indicating I appreciated his compassion. And like that, he was gone. As quickly as he came, he had left. The detective, although through no fault of his own, had devastated me. I was distraught. I couldn't think. I couldn't concentrate. I had one singular thought, *this wasn't happening to me.* My father couldn't be dead. It was impossible; I had just seen him the night before.

I sat and cried; I didn't know what else to do. I silently thanked God that Kalani was visiting her father and not there to witness my breakdown. On top of that, I was clueless as to how I would tell her that she would never see her grandfather again. Sadly she wasn't the only person to which I had to deliver the devastating news.

I composed myself as best as I could and called Charles. As soon as he answered, I burst into tears, and through my sniffles, I said, "Charles, Dad died." He took the news as I had expected; like me, he was devastated. But he collected himself enough to leave work and to join me at my house. While I waited the thirty minutes that it would take for him to arrive, I delivered the news to a few others. I attempted to call my mother but fell short when I remembered I still didn't have her new number. I then called one of my aunts and my grandmother. Both calls went to voicemail; therefore I left messages urging them to have my mother call me. About thirty minutes later my phone rang with a call from a private number. I warily answered the call under the assumption it was my mother; I was correct. Her first words to me were, "What do you want?"

I relayed the news of my father's death to her. It was only my second time doing it, but I was already tired of telling the story. Each time I did, I had to relive the pain as if the detective was still in my living room telling me the news for the first time. In a show of support, my mother, just as Charles had before her, told me she was on her way to be with me. My mother also offered to call Jayson; which was a relief. I didn't have the energy to once again be the bearer of bad news.

While I waited for my brother and mother to arrive, I sat in silence and cried. Regardless of how hard I attempted to process my new reality, I couldn't believe what was happening. After years of a strained relationship, God had seen fit to bring my father and me back together. And although I mourned for what I had lost, I was grateful to be able to live with him in his final year. It was only through the grace of God that I had the time I did and, just like that, it had ended. It felt like a bad dream, and I tried my damnedest to wake up. I longed to hear my father's voice once more. My only recourse was to call his cell phone. I deliberately dialed each digit of his number, praying with each press my father would answer. His phone rang five times and went to voicemail.

"Hey, you've reached Charles Barlow, leave a message at the beep." Being old-fashioned, my father wasn't very adept with technology, and his voicemail greeting proved it. Just before the message ended, it quieted for a few seconds. Then right before the beep, my father's muffled voice could be heard swearing his frustrations while he tried to efficiently navigate the voicemail prompts. Then silence. My father had the same voicemail for years. He never changed it, and no one ever said anything about it. I chuckled through my fallen tears. My father was the funniest person I knew, and he was always able to make me laugh. He hadn't been gone a full day, and I missed him terribly. The most agonizing part of it all was there was nothing I could do to change anything. He wasn't coming back. The permanence of it took my strength; therefore I did the only thing I could. I sat in silence and waited for my mother and brother.

My mother was the first to arrive. She walked in, and the first thing she said was, "Oh Aleesha, you guys didn't just make this up to get me here?"

I contorted my face in confusion. "Why would we do that?"

She explained that she thought my call may have been a ploy for my father and me to attack her. I stared at her, incredulous at the thought that I would lie about the death of my father just so I could bring bodily harm to her. I had no words to sufficiently respond to her asinine statement, I could only confirm that my father had passed away. With that, the truth finally sank in.

A short time later, Charles and Jayson arrived. For each of our own reasons, an air of discomfort surrounded us as we sat awkwardly in the kitchen. I was the first to break the uncomfortable silence. I informed them all that

I was leaving to view the location where my father died. No one else made a move to join me, so I left; alone.

Everyone may have not understood, but I was inexplicably compelled to see where he had taken his last breath. He was my father. I owed it to him. I drove five minutes up the road in the direction the detective indicated. Sure enough, I found the tree. It was broken in half and looked as if it had been struck by lightning. Scattered pieces of my father's bright gold PT Cruiser covered the surrounding area; his license place sat at the base of the tree. The sight of it all infuriated me. Why hadn't the scene been cleaned?

I stood without a sound and took the scene in. I smiled, ever so slightly, at a piece of the gold wreckage. I had always teased my father that his car was a "woman's car"; naturally he insisted otherwise. However, each time I saw a Gold PT Cruiser, I looked to see who was driving and it was always a woman. Although I was surrounded by destruction, the memory sustained me and brought me a sliver of joy while I picked up the remains of what was once my father's car.

While I cleaned, my attention was drawn to fragments strewn beneath the trunk of the broken tree. Beneath the dirt, I found the left lens of my father's eyeglasses. A pang of sadness struck me as I placed it over my eye hoping to see my father's last moments. I wanted to know what he was thinking and what he felt. Was he scared or despite the detective saying he died on impact, did he fight for his life. I wanted answers; I got none. I did, however, feel that my father's presence was there just a few hours earlier, and his energy enveloped me. It was strong and unmistakable. I couldn't contain myself and released a series of heart-wrenching wails at the top of my lungs. Why did he have to leave me? There was much more for us to accomplish.

I stayed at the scene for about an hour. I put the pieces of my father's car in the back of my truck and drove home, where I shared what I saw and the pieces I had collected with my mother and brothers.

At the night's end, I walked aimlessly through the empty house half-expecting the front door to open at any time and my father to walk in. He did not. Thankfully, I was not alone. Charles took a leave of absence from work and stayed with Kalani and me. Having his company was nice.

That night I resolved to dedicate the *Tell Somebody* movement to my father. After all, he was one of the driving forces behind its creation. I vowed to make him proud of me every day, from that day forward. I would not stop until *Tell Somebody* reached victims across the globe.

# CHAPTER ELEVEN

It is often said that when something happens to you, you have three choices; you can let it define you, destroy you, or strengthen you. I choose the latter. One of the greatest tragedies in the death of a loved one is that, irrespective of how much you miss them or how big a hole their absence leaves, life goes on. The world around doesn't stop. Therefore you're put in the position of mourning a great loss while having to simultaneously live in the present and plan for the future.

I wish I could have handled my father's death as well as my five-year-old Kalani. When I told she innocently replied, "Aww man, no more Monday bean night." Anyone within earshot would have incorrectly assumed that she cared more for her dinner than her grandfather. But that was the furthest thing from the truth. Monday bean night, was a weekly ritual my father shared with us. He would lovingly prepare a delicious pot of smoked meat and beans for Kalani and me. It was a humble meal, but something that he always wanted Kalani to remember him by. He succeeded.

Two days after my father's passing my mother, Charles and I went to the funeral home to make the arrangements for his service. While we discussed the particulars of his funeral, it came to my attention that my father's body was in the back room. I had to see him just once more. The funeral director, having seen my father, strongly suggested that I not allow my final memories be of him in the state he was in. I was not deterred. I didn't care what he looked like, he was still my father. I persisted, and the funeral director remained steadfast. In the end, I yielded to his advice; and returned my focus to preparing my father for his final rest.

After all of the particulars were finalized, I was left feeling like I was saying goodbye to my father and I didn't want that. He would always be with me and would always be part of me, but I wanted something tangible to hold on to once he was in his final resting place. So I purchased a silver necklace, on which hung a charm with my father's name, birthstone, and fingerprint. Moving forward, I knew there would be difficult days where I would need my father; this was without question. And although he couldn't physically be with me, I could touch my necklace and find strength in knowing he was, in fact, with me.

On April 6, 2015, my father's wake was held in Fairfield, California. Friends, family, and co-workers gathered to pay their respects and remember my father. One by one, those who wanted to share memories of him came forward. When it was my turn, I stood resolutely before the crowd, wearing a *Tell Somebody* t-shirt. Before I spoke my first word, I glanced at my father who was also wearing a *Tell Somebody* t-shirt. Burying him in his shirt was a no-brainer. If it weren't for him and his advice, *Tell Somebody* may not have been what it was.

I lifted my gaze, confident that my father was proud of me, grabbed the microphone and told everyone my truth; starting with his t-shirt. I let all of those who silently questioned his atypical dress know that my father wore his t-shirt because I was molested as a child. And although it had taken me twenty years to tell him, when I finally did, he helped me launch my *Tell Somebody* movement. My gaze returned to my father, and then back to the crowd before I resumed speaking. I confessed that his death had strengthened me and because of unwavering support there was no way I would let him down. All those who were there bore witness as I swore to dedicate one hundred and fifty percent, to ensure I made him as proud in death as he was of me in life. At the conclusion of my speech, I walked back to my seat contented with my vow to my father.

The warmth, numerous cards, and sincere condolences I received from loved ones, friends and strangers alike, were breathtakingly overwhelming. The love and respect they had for my father were evident in the beautiful flower arrangements that adorned the space around his casket. I was immensely appreciative of it all. But when everyone left I took the flowers and the beautifully written cards home where I was met with silence. I entered my empty four bedroom home with an arm full of offerings and nothing else but the memories of my father. I walked past his bedroom door. I wanted to open the door. I wanted to peek inside for a glimpse of what life was like just one week prior, but I couldn't. In life my father never wanted us to go into his room, and I always respected his wishes. I did the same for him, in death. For as much as I wanted that one last look, I couldn't defy him. To avoid the temptation, I chose to stay on the opposite side of the house.

Two days later, Charles, Kalani and I flew to Grand Coteau, Louisiana, where my father's funeral was to be held. The morning of April 9, I woke up in his family's home, ready to lay him to rest. As I entered the bathroom to prepare for the day, I overheard a muffled conversation where one of the participants expressed their desire for me not to wear "that *Tell Somebody* shirt." The day belonged to my father; therefore, I refused to act out of line. I let their words roll off of my back and dressed without so much as acknowledging what I heard. When they saw us, no one said anything to me, and I made a conscious effort to do the same. We then separated into our designated cars and drove to the church.

Before the funeral began, there was time for friends and family to view my father's body. Since I had already seen him at the wake a few days prior, I took the opportunity to document the day for posterity. Using my cell phone, I filmed everything, the outside of the church, the green grass, and the cows. After which I went inside to pay my final respects.

The moment his service began, I could sense that my father's immediate family had taken issue with the way I dressed my father. They might not have known it, but I put a lot of thought into his attire. When he was about eighteen, my father joined the Air Force. His everyday look consisted of either his Air Force sweat suit or a sweat suit in general. He simply enjoyed wearing them, and would often buy them five at a time, all in different colors. That was the primary deciding factor in my choice for him to be buried in his blue Air Force sweatsuit. I accompanied it with a black *Tell Somebody* t-shirt because of his connection to the movement.

No one said anything directly to me about his outfit, but it was clear they didn't like it. At one point, I noticed that my father's Air Force jacket was zipped up just far enough to cover the words "Tell Somebody" on his shirt. I was too frustrated and appalled to cry, so I unzipped his jacket and returned to my seat to mourn in silence.

At the conclusion of his service, mourners followed the hearse to the gravesite, where my father would be buried just a few feet away from his parents. I, again, pulled out my cell phone and captured every minor detail as we drove through the cemetery. I etched the scene in my mind; still, I needed the video. I didn't want to take the chance of not being able to recall that day. When the preacher spoke his final words, a representative of the Air Force presented me with my father's burial flag in honor of his military service. I held the flag tightly and wept. My tears were for my father, who didn't get the long life he deserved. And they were for me because I had to live without him. I was proud to call him my father. He did so many good things in his life, and his heart was remarkably pure; the flag I held was proof of that.

When it was over everyone went their separate ways; however, Charles, Kalani and I stayed. We watched as he was interred and did not leave until his headstone was cemented in place. The finality of it all put me at ease.

For the duration of my stay in Louisiana, my father's family was less than welcoming, and I experienced very little of the southern hospitality the state was known for. At a time where I would have needed them most, I began to feel like neither my maternal or paternal families were there for me. The only person who showed compassion for me was Charles' maternal uncle. He wasn't even technically related to me and still treated me better than my own family. I know my father would have been mortified, ashamed and disappointed by the treatment I received from his family.

By the morning of our third day in Louisiana, we had officially worn out our welcome. Thankfully we were scheduled to leave anyway. Of all the relatives, only my aunt stayed to see us off. Just before I walked out the door for the last time, I turned to my aunt and said to her, "I overheard that you didn't like some of the things that I decided to do for my dad's funeral. For example, you didn't like that I recorded the event, you and a couple of other family members didn't approve of how I had my dad dressed because y'all thought I should of have had him in a four-piece suit. I also heard that because he was buried in a *Tell Somebody* t-shirt and his Air Force sweat suit he would be the laughing stock of the town!"

I couldn't hold back. Everything I heard and felt over the past few days spilled forth. I continued, "I heard that you said that as far as my *Tell Somebody* movement, there is a time and a place for everything. And the funeral was neither the time nor the place for it, so that's why you zipped up my father's jacket a couple of times during the funeral!"

I wasn't finished. I explained that my father helped me start the movement because he also wanted to save children from sexual abuse. My aunt may have assumed otherwise, but my father would have been proud to be buried in that shirt.

Despite days of behavior that supported everything I said, my aunt denied everything. I didn't have the energy to listen to her lies. Content having said everything I wanted to, I walked out, got in the car and drove off.

The three of us flew home, and the following day I received a call from another one of my aunts. Of course, the call was ridiculous. She wanted to know what my issue was with her and the rest of the family. Needless to say, I voiced each and every one of my grievances, including how going shopping and to the casino with money she claimed not to have to help with funeral arrangements, was more important than her family. When she couldn't stand anymore, she cut me off and said, "Lose my number, you ain't never got to call me again!" before hanging up on me.

I was livid. But sadly it was a feeling I had grown to expect. It wasn't the first time that a family member disowned me because of my truth. I was full of rage and needed an outlet. I made a status update documenting the events of the past few days and tagged her before posting it to my social media account. Regret immediately came over me; I was better than that. I wasn't going to let anger turn me into someone that I wasn't, so I deleted it. In its place, I created and posted a video communicating that when a person tells their story, whatever it may be, they may be disowned by family and friends. I encouraged viewers, should it ever happen to them, to be strong and not let it destroy them or defeat them from their ultimate goal.

I expressed that by forming *Tell Somebody,* I had been disowned, argued with, hung up on and so much more from both sides of my family. I was told to get over it, deal with it, it wasn't the right time to talk, and I was lying. It's hard to hear those things, particularly from family. However, their reaction to me indicated that I was more powerful than I realized. If I was capable of stirring emotions and creating conversations with others as I had with family, I could not be stopped. Although I would be met with resistance along the way, I wanted to ignite feelings in survivors that inspired them to fight for themselves. I wanted to elicit shame and guilt in those who abused children and encourage them to turn themselves into the authorities, seek help and refrain from predatory behaviors. I had discovered my new power, and I wouldn't trade it for anything or anyone in the world. I was doing God's work, and if someone didn't understand, then I had no place for them in my life.

My light was bright and glowing for all to see. The setbacks with my family were a minor inconvenience. With God by my side, I knew I was going to be able to distance myself from negative vibes, negative people, and negative energy. Little did the world know, I was prepared for an uphill battle and could handle whatever would come my way. I had the will to fight and be the example to others that healing was possible.

# CHAPTER TWELVE

In the wake of my father's funeral, I redoubled my efforts to *Tell Somebody*. Whereas I could have let his death derail the movement, instead I chose to use it as motivation to reach bigger and better heights. I owed it to him to keep fighting. For inspiration, I would look back on the videos he made for the movement, especially the one we never got to redo. The impromptu nature of it caught his raw essence, and his words rang truer than ever. I would playback the video and listen as if it was the first time. His voice would resonate through the speakers, "Aleesha, keep doing what you're doing. Keep advocating because somebody has to do it. I'm so proud of you." His words were all I needed to motivate me to go harder.

I resumed my letter writing campaign to influential television shows and networks, including *Dr. Phil*, *Steve Harvey*, and the Oprah Winfrey network. Likewise, I sent messages to celebrities by way of Instagram and Twitter introducing myself and telling my story. I would further inform them of the *Tell Somebody* movement and offer to send them a t-shirt with the hopes they would support the cause. I put forth so much effort that my social media accounts would block my activity under the assumption I was spamming other accounts. Eventually, my dedication paid off. On April 22, 2015, Karrine Steffans was the first celebrity to write me back. She was moved by my words and graciously accepted my offer for a *Tell Somebody* t-shirt. Receiving her response was the confirmation that I needed. If I could get through to one celebrity, then I was confident that I could get the attention of others.

Since I had begun to dedicate a large portion of my time to social media outreach and letter writing, I wanted to be sure that I wasn't neglecting my supporters. To prevent such a thing, I came up with *Tell Somebody Interviews*. The purpose of these interviews was to highlight survivors speaking out about past or present sexual abuse, to inspire others to do the same.

On May 23, 2015, I taped Season 1 Episode 1 of the *Tell Somebody Interviews* in the same park that I held my barbecue two months prior. There was no rhyme or reason to how I picked my first interviewee; I simply approached the first person I saw. She was an older Caucasian woman who was setting up a face painting booth for a child's birthday party. I politely walked up to her, and I said, "As a child, I was molested and was told to keep it a secret. I was wondering if you were molested as a child, and if so would you be willing to share your story for my series?" She replied yes to both questions and correspondingly I began recording.

"I was molested by a male teacher growing up," she began. I listened silently as she spoke about how her teacher would put his hands up her shirt and fondle her breast. She continued on to say that when she reported the abuse, her principal told her that she would be the one in trouble because no one would believe her claim. So she didn't tell. The abuse she suffered at the hands of someone she trusted affected well beyond school age. As a result, she had just learned to read at the age of sixty. Coupled with her apathetic principal, her teacher's predatory behavior turned her away from school.

At the conclusion of her story, the woman buried her face in her hands and wept. I couldn't help but cry with her. She wiped away her tears and exhaled the hurt that lingered after decades. After regaining her composure, she shared that she was in the process of writing her first book on the subject. Although we had just met, I was exceptionally proud of her. Before parting ways, we exchanged information. A few months later, she contacted me, and we met up at a Starbucks where she interviewed me for her upcoming book.

The second interview on the first episode of the *Tell Somebody Interviews* featured my brother Charles opening up with details of his past sexual abuse. When he was seven or eight-years-old, he was sent by his mother to live with a friend who owned a nursing home. While living with the friend, Charles was regularly molested by her fifteen-year-old granddaughters. Thankfully, he was rescued from his abusive situation when our father, who had been searching for him, was rewarded custody. After that, Charles lived with our father and was never abused again. While in the middle of recounting his past, something he said troubled me. "Well I'm a boy, so was I really being molested?" he openly pondered.

His question deeply disturbed me. I wondered how many others thought like Charles, and identified it as the rationale why many boys and men didn't come forward. I couldn't help myself; I had to shed some light on his faulty concept of sexual abuse. I used a tactic similar to that my father used on me in earlier times. I asked how he would feel if an older girl was molesting his son. And just as our father's words put my abuse into perspective, mine did the same for Charles.

His story was touching in so many ways and gave an often overlooked male perspective of being molested by a female. I was grateful he shared it with my viewers and the impact it had, along with other interviews, was remarkable. Each time a survivor shared their story, another survivor realized they weren't alone.

In May of 2015, I took a short break from the *Tell Somebody Interviews* to reprioritize my life. At that point,

I no longer had the benefit of my older brother living with me. He had since returned to his home an hour and a half away. It was just Kalani and I living in a four bedroom house; although I wasn't sure how much longer we would be there. My mother was in the process of putting it on the market.

In the meantime, my father's life insurance policy paid out, and my mother had given me a portion of it. I had no plans of wasting any of that money. I was living in my father's house rent-free until it sold and for the first time in my life, I was going to invest in myself.

Every weekend, while Kalani was with her father, I would wake up at six in the morning and drive six hours from Fairfield to Los Angles. Upon my arrival, I would check into a hotel, shower, and grab something to eat before getting dressed and heading to local events. I met Russell Simmons, Matt Barnes, Affion Crockett, and Laura Govan at various events. Laura Govan was very kind, and her vulnerability touched me when she revealed her own story of being molested on *Iyanla: Fix My life*. When her episode aired, I was remarkably proud to see that another victim found their voice to speak out.

I engaged with countless other celebrities, including Bay Area natives rapper Too Short and Zendaya. I also met apl.de.ap, of Black Eyed Peas, Omarion and Fizz of B2K, Flo-rida, Musiq Soulchild, Tinashe, Trae tha Truth and the Ying Yang Twins just to name a few. I told them my story, we took pictures, and I gifted some of them with *Tell Somebody* t-shirts. In many cases, we also exchanged contact information. I sincerely appreciated each and every one of them for taking the time to hear me out. Their genuine support fuelled me.

At the end of each weekend, which typically ended around three in the morning, I would return to my hotel for a few hours of sleep before taking the six-hour trip back to Fairfield. I would be exhausted, but I was more determined. *Tell Somebody* sustained me. I knew without any doubt that in spite of the blood, sweat, and tears, my hard work would pay off. Therefore, I kept going. I made the six-hour trip from Los Angeles to Fairfield and back, every weekend, for six months straight.

I began to reap the fruits of my labor on July 12, 2015. That morning I woke up to a multitude of new Facebook friends. While I slept, comedian and actor, D.L. Hughley shared a photo of me and about twenty others, all wearing our *Tell Somebody* t-shirts. He shared the photo, which just so happened to be the background image for the *Tell Somebody* website, with the caption explaining that I was sexually abused as a child and needed help to continue the fight against child molestation. The acknowledgment I received from him and others, confirmed that I was on the right path. God was opening doors for me, and I walked through each newly opened door with a purposeful stride.

On July 22, 2015, which was coincidentally Kalani's sixth birthday, I was asked to speak at the *Pink Panther*

*Sorority Self-Esteem Camp*, in Oakland. I was honored to work with the non-profit organization because it supports a cause dear to my heart. It encourages and promotes self-love to young black girls as a way of fostering healthy self-esteem. I was immensely excited to participate in such a wonderful event, especially since it was Kalani's birthday and we would share the experience together. I loved that my daughter chose to be hands-on with the movement. It warmed my heart to see that she enjoyed every minute of being by my side to watch everything I did and hear everything I said.

That year we spent her birthday doing our best to prevent participants of the *Pink Panther Sorority Self-Esteem Camp* from becoming a statistic. Data indicated that ten of the thirty girls I spoke to that day were or would become a victim of child sexual abuse. I wanted to do all I could to not let that happen, and I knew the first step was education. First I taught them about their bodies and demonstrated what parts were off limits for others, whether they were strangers, family or friends. I told them what happened to me when I was their age and about the *Tell Somebody* movement. Near the conclusion of my lecture, I passed out *Tell Somebody* hats, which they were pleased to have. Many were so happy they put the hats on right away. Then they did something awesome. They surprised Kalani with cupcakes and serenaded her with *Happy Birthday*.

I left the *Pink Panther Sorority Self-Esteem Camp* with my chest puffed out with pride. I had equipped those children with the knowledge to empower them, and the tools they could use to protect themselves from sexual predators. It was the type of service that healed the scars my grandfather had left behind. I had found my purpose and was actively living it. That day when I left the camp, I realized that the work I had just done was why God put me on Earth. I was to give strength to survivors and interview them, and I was to educate children and parents about sexual abuse.

In the beginning, when I first posted outreach videos, someone wrote to me and chastised me for my daughter's involvement in *Tell Somebody*. They were of the opinion that Kalani was too young to be an advocate for sexual abuse victims because she supposedly didn't know what molestation was. I kindly let them know that she was actually the perfect age and was fully aware of what molestation is. And that, in part, was one of the obstacles I was up against. People didn't want to talk to their children about a topic as sensitive as sexual abuse because of the assumption that they were too young to understand. My daughter was six, which was around the age that my grandfather began touching me. I would have loved if someone had spoken to me about sexual abuse, the biggest tragedy of my childhood could have been avoided if someone had. But since I was never taught, I suffered for years. I didn't want that for my child or any other child.

That was just one of the hundreds of emails and messages I received daily. And while some were of the same tone, most were from people who appreciated what I was doing. I tried my best to respond to each and every person, and in the cases where the written word wasn't enough, we exchanged phone numbers. I had no qualms about sitting on the phone for hours if it meant I could help someone by listening and offering encouraging words.

During the summer of 2015, a college student, who had been raped, reached out to me. She told me she was to deliver an impact statement at her rapist's sentencing and wanted to wear a *Tell Somebody* t-shirt while doing so. I, without hesitation, sent her a shirt and went one step further. I asked if I could accompany her to the sentencing to support the reading of her impact statement. She graciously said yes. I was dedicated to being there for her. So much so, after attending previously scheduled events the night before, I woke up at five in the morning and drove four and a half hours to the designated courthouse. Our connection was instant.

I watched her in that courtroom standing unashamedly in her *Tell Somebody* t-shirt and graduation cap. Her rapist wouldn't even look at her. He kept his head down and back to her the entire time. His posture said it all, and I loved that she had taken her power back from him. I watched the young lady and listened closely as she spoke. She told him that even though he refused to face her, she wanted him to know she was wearing a shirt that read *Tell Somebody* across the front and it meant exactly what it said. We were going to stop sick people like him who preyed on others for their own sick desires. The young lady went on to say that her rapist had indeed hurt her, but she was not going to live in pain anymore; he was no longer going to have a hold on her life. She was breaking free from his bonds and accomplishing a list of goals she had set for herself, including graduating from college.

I was so happy for her that my emotions got the best of me and I wept silently. She was a powerful sight to behold, and I played a part in the strength she displayed. After a few formalities, the judge sentenced her rapist, and right before we left he thanked everyone who came to support the young lady. He even expressed his sentiments about my movement, which let me know he respected what I was doing and why I was doing it.

# CHAPTER THIRTEEN

In the weeks after I accompanied the young lady to court, word of *Tell Somebody* continued to spread. On September 16, 2015, *Blackdoctor.org*, a trusted resource for healthy lifestyle information, contacted me and requested an interview. It goes without saying that I obliged. I was honored that a website known for tackling issues prevalent in the African- American community found my movement worthy of discussion and placement on their website.

About a week later, on the twenty-second of September, I awakened from my sleep at five in the morning. It was none other than God, and he said to me, "Go write Oprah." The message was too clear to ignore. I got out of bed, logged into my social media account and went to her page. My message was brief and to the point. It read, "Oprah mark my words, one day we will work together. My name is Aleesha Barlow, and I created the Tell Somebody movement. I'm a survivor of child abuse, and all I want to do is help others that are going through or have gone through any form of sexual abuse."

Eight minutes later I received a response. "You are a perfect role model for turning pain into power!" it said.

I was beyond thrilled! Oprah Winfrey had not only responded to me, but she complimented me and offered words of encouragement. Her reply, though eleven simple words, reinforced my conviction that she and I would inevitably work together to carry out the message of *Tell Somebody*.

On the day of my father's birthday, September 26, 2015, I had my first big speaking engagement at a women's conference in Houston, Texas. It was exhilarating to be able to share my big moment with him in spirit.

While in Texas, I had the fortune of visiting my father's younger sister and her son, who had migrated to Texas from Louisiana after Hurricane Katrina. Much to my delight, they both came to hear me speak at the conference. It was a beautiful thing to look out into the audience and be greeted by the warm and loving faces of family; all while my father looked down at me from above.

Later that evening, after the conference had ended, my family and I decided to honor my father. Together we purchased balloons and found a secluded area where we held a simple private ceremony for him. We released the balloons, and they floated into the heavens while we spoke of his beautiful soul and sang *Happy Birthday*. It was the perfect way to end the day.

In early October, A Plus, a digital media company founded by actor Ashton Kutcher, featured me and *Tell Somebody* on their website. Everything was steadily falling into place, and I was thankful for every opportunity to tell my story that came my way.

Interview requests and messages, from survivors and supporters, alike had long confirmed that connection people had to the *Tell Somebody* movement. However, it was a real eye-opener when on November 21, 2015, someone sent me a photo of "Tell Somebody" tattooed on their wrist. It was an amazing sight, and it inspired me to express my devotion to the cause in the same manner. I left immediately for my local tattoo shop. I arrived to find that it was closing in forty-five minutes, and I was initially turned away. But I begged the tattoo artist and pointed out that my request was for a simple tattoo. Ultimately she gave into my appeal and tattooed the words "Tell Somebody" across my collarbone.

While she worked, we discussed God, church and among other things how she led Bible study. The timing of receiving the photo and arriving at the tattoo shop, aligned perfectly as I realized I was where I needed to be when I needed to be there. I was at a time in my life where I was slowly getting to know God. I had been praying and learning Him on my own, but I was at the point where I wanted to be a part of a church community to be around other positive people. I gladly accepted the tattoo artist's invitation to attend her church, which I have attended ever since.

Eventually, my life slowed down a bit. With the newfound free time on my hands, I returned to conducting my *Tell Somebody Interviews*. Each interview always opened with the same questions: "Have you ever been sexually abused?" and "What are you doing to cope with the pain?" One of my favorite *Tell Somebody* episodes was Season 1's Episode 3, filmed in Hollywood. While conducting interviews, I came across an older African-American woman waiting for the bus to arrive. She and I struck up a conversation, and I began to tell her my story of sexual abuse. I paused for a split second to rephrase a particular question I was prepared to ask when she interjected and asked, "Have you healed from it?"

I truthfully answered, "Yeah, I'm healed by talking to people." I then asked, "Did something happen to you? Are you healed?"

The woman turned to look for her bus and replied, "Yeah, it was a babysitter." She became a bit flustered as she corrected herself to say the babysitter actually didn't know. It was the babysitter's grandson that violated her. He used to touch her underneath her clothes; however, at the time it was happening she didn't know his actions constituted molestation. Her bus pulled up, and she expressed that she had to leave.

As she ran away, I called out one last question, "Did you ever tell anybody?"

She turned around, looked over her shoulder in my direction and yelled back, "You! You're the first person I've told!"

My mouth dropped in apparent shock. She was exactly who I wanted to reach with my interviews. I wanted the interviews to serve as a safe place for survivors to lay down their burdens and tell their truth, whether it was their first time speaking about it or not. I was deeply moved that after decades of holding her secret, the woman felt safe enough in my presence to share it with my viewers.

Although Season 1 Episode 3 was my favorite *Tell Somebody Interview*, my most important interview was filmed with my mother and aunt on November 25, 2015; Thanksgiving Day. In her efforts to sell my father's house my mother would frequently visit, and over time we slowly began to rebuild our relationship. During one of her many visits, I explained the purpose of *Tell Somebody* and showed her what I was doing with the movement. Being as we weren't in contact prior to that time, everything was new to her. She didn't even know that I had been on the news. I showed her a clip of my appearance and many of the personal messages that people wrote to me. I wanted her to see all the people that I helped along my journey of healing. She began to see the bigger picture and realized that *Tell Somebody* was bigger than our family. It was bigger than the arguments, misunderstandings, and miscommunications; bigger than the secrets, deceit, and lies. She finally came to understand that it was about saving and helping.

In the interim, *Dr. Phil* emailed me again and asked if any of my family members had a change of heart about appearing on the show. I threw caution to the wind and asked my mother and aunt if they wanted to appear on *Dr. Phil* with me. They both hesitated. Seeing that my mother had successfully sold my father's house and planned to move to Hawaii within the month, I figured her answer would be no. Still, I wanted an answer. The weight of their hesitation hung heavily in the air. I rescued them both from the awkward uneasiness that permeated the room before they offered the excuses I could practically see dripping from the tips of their tongues. I told them that if they wouldn't appear on *Dr. Phil*, then they could at least allow me to interview them for an episode of *Tell Somebody*. They both agreed.

The three of us sat in my aunt's guest bedroom and with the camera rolling my aunt and mother told their stories. They both openly admitted that their grandfather had abused them just as mine had me. They too were told by their mother, to keep it a secret and in a story that mirrored my own, the abuse continued. My mother and aunt also vaguely remember their father, my grandfather, touching them as kids. The topic of their interview then shifted to me.

My mother began to speak, and I recognized her words as the same ones she first spoke when my father and I initially confronted her about my abuse. Once again she professed her belief that my grandfather had stopped abusing me after she and my aunts talked to him. Since I never mentioned it again, she had no reason to believe that he hadn't stopped. My mother maintained that if she had known the abuse was continuing, she would have put a stop to it. When she originally said those exact words, I didn't believe her, but as the saying goes time heals all wounds. That night, I believed her.

Much like my mother, my aunt reiterated her words from the first time I challenged her for not saving me from my grandfather. She shared how she invited me into her home and comforted me. She even spoke again of how she threatened to send my grandfather to prison if he ever touched me again. Capturing her words on film was nice.

After each of them finished their own stories and the roles they play in mine, they both gave heartfelt apologies for not doing more to save me. I wanted to ask more questions, particularly since the revelation that they were told by a loved one, just as I was, to keep their abuse a secret. But I didn't want to go backward. Besides, my fight was no longer with them; my fight was with the man who abused me for years, my grandfather. I could finally see how much it hurt them to have to live with the fact that they didn't do more to help me. I saw no reason to turn the knife in their wound. I made the conscious choice to accept their truths, as well as their apologies, and begin to heal; together.

We ended the video with a special message to parents telling them to *do* something as soon as a child comes forward about sexual abuse. The message additionally included encouraging words to survivors. Then all three of us, wearing our *Tell Somebody* t-shirts, took a picture together which marked my mother and aunt's enlistment in my movement. It pleased me to no end that they were finally taking accountability for their actions. With everything out in the open, we were finally able to close a very painful chapter of our lives and move forward with our lives.

Where I was in high spirits about reuniting with my mother and aunt, many of my supporters weren't happy with our reunion. After I posted their interview and the picture we took together, I received countless comments questioning my choice to forgive them. It was unsettling that they were actually angry. I found it difficult to believe that after all of the love and support I had given my supporters, many would take issue with how I chose to heal. Instead of getting angry, I explained to them my concept of forgiveness and how forgiving those who had wronged me was for my benefit, not theirs. I wanted to heal; therefore, I couldn't hold on to what they did. I had long accepted that I couldn't control how others treated me; I could only control how I let it affect me. The first half of my life, my entire childhood, was taken from me and I had no plans of giving anyone the rest of my life. If I didn't forgive them, and let God handle everything, then I would have relinquished total control of my life.

That's the beauty of the power that lies in the words "Tell Somebody." We have to stop holding onto secrets to protect others. We must get it off of our chests and forgive, so as not to let hurt, pain, guilt or shame consume our lives. We have to tell somebody to take back our lives and release negative energy to live each new day to its fullest.

# CHAPTER FOURTEEN

At the beginning of 2016, my mother officially moved to Hawaii, and I was ready to begin the next chapter of my life and the *Tell Somebody* movement. Taking into account that I had forgiven my mother and aunt, there was nothing left to hold me back. On February 20, I produced *A Letter to Child Molesters*, a powerful two-minute video starring Kalani in the role of a young Aleesha, and me appearing as myself. Where in the past, my videos were directed at abuse survivors, *A Letter to Child Molesters*, was intended specifically for those who preyed upon children. I envisioned it as a direct conversation with child molesters, a public service announcement of sorts, where the ultimate message was simple: "Please Stop."

## END SILENCED ABUSE: TELL SOMEBODY

Before posting it online, I prayed that it would reach its intended audience. I didn't want another innocent child to experience my incomprehensible reality. I hoped that pedophiles truly listened to the words Kalani and I spoke, and realized the lasting damage inflicted upon victims by their vile acts. And I wanted anyone who saw the error of their ways after watching the video to seek professional help and change their predatory behavior.

Later that month, my uncle, who was formerly married to my mother's youngest sister, contacted me and asked if I would send him a *Tell Somebody* shirt. It was my pleasure to do so, and I sent him one right away. In the course of our conversation, he expressed how proud he was of me for being so forthcoming with a topic that many would try their hardest to forget. I reveled in the compliments.

Then to my surprise, in an act that went over and beyond my expectations, he sent me a video. In it, he admitted that he knew that my grandfather was abusing me as a child. He went on to say that although he wanted to tell my father and physically punish my grandfather, loyalty to his wife, and her request to keep quiet, compelled him to remain silent. For years, he was weighed down by regret and guilt over his decision. To an extent, his video was his atonement for his part in allowing my molestation to continue. His bravery was compelling, as I watched his confession over and over. I commended him for his strength and thanked him repeatedly for his numerous apologies. With his permission I posted his video, letting the world see the widespread effects of keeping child sexual abuse a secret. It is not only obviously damning to the child but it takes a significant toll on those who protect the molester with their secrecy as well.

My uncle's confession was further proof that the truth was contagious. The more people who embodied fearlessness and, in turn, spoke out against their abuse, the less protection molesters and abusers were afforded. That is why I told my story and continued to tell it throughout the entire year of 2015. I traveled the world and networked. I spoke at camps and conferences; each time with the hopes of inspiring change. My fan base steadily grew, increasing to over one hundred thousand combined followers across my social media accounts. To have so many watching and supporting was a huge responsibility; one that I gladly accepted and I refused to let them down.

After much thought, it dawned on me that although it was impossible for me to speak directly to each and every victim of child sexual abuse, I could create the platform where their voices could be heard. On March 10, 2016, a young lady sent me a photo of her wearing a *Tell Somebody* t-shirt and holding a sign inscribed with the same message. Attached to the photo was an account of abuse that matched the pain in her eyes. But within her story, there was also hope.

Prior to sending the photo, the young lady had spoken of her sexual abuse at an event. As she addressed the crowd of young children, she repeatedly implored them to, "Tell somebody." I had no doubt of the effect her words had on the audience. I knew their power since the fateful evening my father spoke them to me. It was that same power that motivated two girls to approach the young lady at the end of her speech and reveal that they, too, were victims of sexual abuse. I immediately posted the young lady's photo and story. Just as I had inspired her and as she inspired the girls; I hoped her story would inspire others who happened upon my page. And it did. The very next day, I received another story and photo of a different person holding a sign that read "Tell Somebody."

Every day of 2016 and well into 2017, I posted a different survivor's story. I was tremendously proud of each survivor who was courageous enough to share their story.

Regardless of how many messages I received, nothing could diminish the sincere sense of pride I felt each time someone came forward with their story. There was nothing more rewarding than being told that someone gathered the strength to tell someone they were being or had been abused. There was supreme satisfaction when they pressed charges against their abusers, who then either sat in jail or awaited trial.

In the midst of crusading for child sexual abuse victims, I met the love of my life, and we are engaged to be married. As of August 2017, my fiancé Rail and I have been happily engaged, after being in a relationship for approximately two years. He is the one and only romantic partner who I felt comfortable enough with to confide my history of sexual abuse. And despite my hidden scars, he welcomed me into his life. Rail brought support, compassion, and love into my life. With me, he was patient and understood how my past abuse affected our sexual intimacy. He wasn't ever offended or turned off when I flinched after he touched me sensually or sexually. Rail never judged me nor did it anger him. He is kind and posses the natural inclination to help others and has devoted himself to the *Tell Somebody* movement. He extends himself to the cause in any way he is needed, whether it's by completing paperwork, recording events or manning the grill at *Tell Somebody Barbecues*. He was, and is, truly a blessing.

Rail's support is invaluable, and just by being himself he has brought something to my life that, as someone who had been molested, I didn't think was possible. As an example to others who thought as I once had, Rail and I filmed a video detailing what it was like to be in a relationship with a survivor of child molestation. In it, he delivered a message to other men and women involved with survivors. His message was clear; survivors needed someone who was supportive, patient and kind.

Correspondingly, I conveyed that as survivors, we needed to let our significant others know what we have been through, and foster open dialogue. Together Rail and I stressed the importance of each person being a part of the other's support system.

Just as the videos I previously posted, our relationship video was met with an overall positive response. And as I continued to post videos on varying topics, from bringing awareness to healing, I noticed the number of new followers increased which clearly indicated that I needed to post videos more frequently.

My overall goal was and had always been, to impart to survivors that while healing was possible, it was a lengthy process. I needed them to understand that the effects of abuse would color parts of their lives they would never imagine, and may never fully heal. Long after their anger has subsided, their self-esteem has recovered, and they have mourned the childhood that could have been; a memory, smell or friendly touch could trigger old feelings. Still, there is a purpose to be found in their pain. Survivors, like me, can use their voice to advocate for those who are unable to do it for themselves and their experience to help parents and loved ones spot the signs of molestation before it's too late.

With the help of God and those who loved me, I wasn't going to let anyone or anything stand in the way of me helping as many people as I possibly could before I left the face of the Earth. Nothing, not major setbacks, not minor inconveniences or non-believers would stop me from working tirelessly to get pedophiles off the street. A life of advocacy was written for me, and I was here to fulfill my purpose.

In September 2016, after forming the six-member board required by the State of California, I applied for an Articles of Incorporation to have *Tell Somebody* legally recognized as a corporation. At the time I was without transportation of my own; however, I wasn't going to let that deter me. I determinedly took the one-hour commute to the California Secretary of State's office in Sacramento. When I arrived, I walked confidentially up to the large building, pulled open the double doors and strutted toward the customer service counter with my paperwork and filing fee in hand. I was ecstatic; the feeling was unreal. *Tell Somebody* was on the verge of being an official corporation; a soon to be well-known one at that. I was on top of the world when I boarded the bus for the return trip home. Unfortunately, later that night I discovered a small error on my application and had to repeat the entire trip again the next day. My second attempt was more successful, and my paperwork was filed without a hitch. After much determination, dedication and the grace of God, the State of California deemed *Tell Somebody* a bona fide corporation. I would later go on to file the 501(c)(3) paperwork necessary to be designated a non-profit, tax-exempt organization.

Things were coming together for *Tell Somebody;* however, I didn't let my triumphs distract me from responding to survivors and reaching out to celebrities via social media every day. I was often left in amazement when after receiving my short messages, powerful celebrities believed in my cause enough to follow me. My Instagram account was followed by the likes of Eve, Lil Mama, Alicia Keys, Rosie O'Donnell, and Tom Arnold.

In November of that same year, Claudette Ortiz, formerly of City High, showed her support as the first celebrity to publicly wear a *Tell Somebody* t-shirt. She additionally made a video expressing her support for the movement. It was wonderfully flattering to have her complete support.

With the arrival of the holiday season, I found a way to combine the movement with other philanthropic endeavors. In December 2016, I hosted *Tell Somebody's First Annual Christmas Toy Drive.* In addition to collecting donations, I purchased toys, blankets, and other necessities to help those in need get through the holidays. Together, Kalani and I delivered the items to neighborhood homeless shelters. Two of the local news stations caught wind of the drive and insisted upon interviewing me. I was honored to be recognized by my community, it gave me solace that I was doing something right.

Around the same time, I did a phone interview with Lady Ray of 106 KMEL on iHeartRadio. The interview aired on seven different radio stations throughout the Bay Area. There must have been substantial interest in the message of Tell Somebody, because the interview continued to air well into January 2017. Many of my supporters listened in and sent well-wishes and congratulatory messages.

After my radio interview, I was invited to speak in front of Los Angeles City Hall, where KABC Channel 7 News and others were covering an anti-rape protest. It was overall a great experience, particularly because a special friendship grew from that day. My newfound friend, who was also a victim of sexual abuse, would go on to make an introduction that led to an invitation to speak in front of a very important demographic of my movement: preschoolers.

The day of my speech, I stood before the class of preschoolers concerned whether or not I presented information on child sexual abuse in a manner that was digestible to them. Being as they were younger children, it was imperative that they fully grasped my message. My words were worth nothing if they couldn't understand them. As I concluded my speech, the school's director suggested that I act out a few of the scenarios to give the children a better understanding of my message. It was a brilliant idea, and I fully incorporated it into every future lecture or speech given to children of a certain age.

With the arrival of spring and to commemorate Sexual Abuse Awareness Month, I threw the *First Annual*

# END SILENCED ABUSE: TELL SOMEBODY

*Tell Somebody Easter Egg Hunt* on April 16, 2017. The event was a great opportunity for amusement, education, and prevention. Neighborhood children came out and enjoyed themselves as they hunted Easter eggs for a cause. A lucky few even found golden eggs, for which they were rewarded *Tell Somebody* gear.

More often than not, *Tell Somebody* affords me the opportunity to interact with survivors, like myself, or to focus on prevention. However, there have been occasions where I have been confronted with the heartbreaking reality of children in the midst of abuse. At those times, it's almost unbearable. Of course, I do everything I can to provide any assistance they require, including directing them to the proper authorities. Still, it's harrowing. I know firsthand the pain they are feeling; as well as the anguish and confusion that will come later in life. But if there is one takeaway, it's that *Tell Somebody* inspires them to take a stand against their abusers. The bravery that these children exhibit by coming forward is the reason that I will never stop.

At times my job is hard, frustrating, and distressing, but it is rewarding, wonderful and worthwhile. Though I wouldn't wish young Aleesha's fate on anyone, from my pain, I have gained an immeasurable and dogged determination to fight for me and others. I am only one person; however, that will not dissuade me. If I can help one person, who then goes on to help another, who then continues the trend, then I have succeeded in my purpose.

There are a lot of victims of child sexual abuse, who see death as the only option for escaping their pain. I stand before them as evidence that it is not, and living proof that they can take their life back from the molesters who tried to destroy them. We, survivors, are a band of brothers and sisters, who have experienced what no child should, but we are stronger than any amount of shame or guilt. And we prove that by living, knowing our worth, telling our stories and helping others. Each time I hear that someone is contemplating suicide, I think of what would have become if I had killed myself. All of the people who I have helped and who have gained strength from my movement, would more than likely still be living in silence.

I am grateful to all of those who have allowed me to help them through the years. It is truly a blessing to have come to the aid of survivors from near and far; whether it is as an inspiration, confidant, or example. All I have ever wanted to do is prevent molestation and bring awareness to the warning signs, so no child has to suffer. And in the unfortunate event that a child is already a victim of sexual abuse, I want to instill in them that the right thing to do is always *tell somebody*.

Aleesha, age 12
Family outing at the beach.

Aleesha and Kalani
In front of the tree where Aleesha's father was killed on
March 29, 2015

Aleesha Barlow, creator of the #TellSomebodyMovement, is a survivor of sexual abuse. At the tender age of six, she told her mother and aunts that their father was inappropriately touching her. Not only was Aleesha forced to keep the abuse from the police and her father; the abuse was allowed to continue. Now twenty years later, Aleesha and her young daughter, speak at schools educating young children about their bodies and letting them know to *tell somebody* if they're being hurt. Her ultimate goal is to give strength to other survivors to tell their story to foster healing.

Keep up with Aleesha on social media at Facebook: Leesh Bee, Twitter: @LeeshLSM, Instagram: @_queenleesh @tellsomebodymovement, and her website at *www.itstimetotellsomebody.org*.

Shalonda R. Johnson, professionally known as "SJ," is originally from Hampton, VA. Since the age of fifteen, she has aspired to become a writer and actress. Upon graduation, she left Virginia to study acting at Temple University's extensive Theater Program. In 2007, she received her BA degree in Theater; and has been pursuing her dreams of writing and acting ever since. Her recent works include national commercials for Dr. Miracle's hair care products, Gerber, 5-Hour Energy, Five Below, Beyoncé's video *The Best Thing I Never Had*, and her debut novel Redemption & Repercussions.

Keep up with SJ on social media at Facebook: Shalonda SJ Johnson, Twitter: @sjauthoractress, Instagram: @sjauthoractress, and her website at *www.shalondajohnson.com*.

To learn more about preventing the sexual abuse of children, please contact
Stop It Now! at **413-587-3500**
or visit their website at *www.stopitnow.org.*

If you or someone you know is a victim or survivor of sexual assault, please contact
RAINN (Rape, Abuse & Incest National Network) at
**1-800-656-HOPE (1-800-656.4673)**
or visit their website at.*www.rainn.org.*

If you or someone you know is a victim of child sexual assault or child abuse, please contact the
National Child Abuse Hotline at
**1-800-4-A-Child (1-800-422-4453)**
or visit their website at *www.childhelp.org.*

If you or someone you know would like to support an organization that seeks to end child abuse of any kind, please donate to Tell Somebody at
*www.itstimetotellsomebody.org.*

To book Aleesha Barlow for speaking engagements, school assemblies, and community events, please contact her at **TellSomebodyMGMT@gmail.com.**

CPSIA information can be obtained
at www.ICGtesting.com
Printed in the USA
FSOW01n0239101017
39686FS